Modern Africa

A Captivating Guide to Modern African History

Free Bonus from Captivating History: History Ebook

Hi History Lovers!

My name is Matt Clayton, and I'm the creator of Captivating History. First off, I want to THANK YOU for reading our books in the Captivating History series. As an avid reader of History myself, I aim to produce books that will hold you captive.

Now you have a chance to join our exclusive history list so you can get the ebook below for free as well as discounts and a potential to get more history books for free! Simply click the link below to join.

P.S. If you join now, you will also receive a free Mythology book. Remember that it's 100% free to join the list.

Captivatinghistory.com/ebook

Also, make sure to follow us on Facebook, Twitter and Youtube by searching for Captivating History.

Table of Contents

Introduction

Africa, the second-largest continent on Earth, cuts across 20 percent of the world's total landmass and is home to at least 1.4 billion people. Some say it's the cradle of mankind since we reportedly evolved from a primate order of ancient species.

Vast deserts like the Sahara, lush tropical rainforests like the Congo Basin, high mountains like Kilimanjaro, and endless rivers like the Nile all have a home in Africa, affecting its rich yet understated history.

The history of Africa began long before a pen could be put to paper, but as it stands, the continent is where fifty-four countries have coexisted in equal parts of warm harmony and chilling chaos. More than two thousand languages are spoken in this continent, speaking to the wealth of cultural diversity around which most of the history of Africa revolves. This book will take you on a journey of the continent in modern times and how it overcame the dark ages before an era of the most stability ever seen.

You will be drawn into the theaters of war and the stories of friendship, ambition, betrayal, and rare sacrifices. Whether you are an enthusiast of African history or a curious beginner, this book has carefully selected the most important events in modern African history, key figures, and unforgettable legacies.

After all, as Martin Luther King Jr. once said, "We are made by history."

Chapter 1 – Africa and Slavery

Typically, the mention of the slave trade casts the mind back to the transatlantic slave trade, which lasted from the 16th to the 19th century. While this period in African history radically reshaped the lives of millions of natives and cannot be underemphasized, slavery had existed in the continent long before the Europeans came.

Ancient Africa was home to many expanding empires and kingdoms and, like the rest of the world, had highly stratified societies. A person's wealth depended on a number of factors, including how many slaves they owned. This was an indigenous form of slavery that would eventually be overshadowed by export slavery beginning in the 7th century.

In ancient Africa, not every slave was born a slave. A common occurrence, especially in West Africa, was debt slavery, where a person (usually a woman or child) was used as debt collateral. Until the debt was fully repaid, the borrower would hold the human collateral captive. In the event that the debtor died before repaying his debt or became permanently unable to repay, the human collateral remained the property of the borrower. This is why the "loan sharks" of ancient Africa were notorious slave-owners.

An expose by a Scottish explorer of West Africa, Mungo Park, gave some more insight into the nature of slavery in ancient Africa. In his bestseller book *Travels in the Interior Districts of Africa*, Mungo Park described three categories of slaves and their realities:

"The slaves in Africa, I suppose, are nearly in the proportion of three to one to the freemen. They claim no reward for their services except food and clothing and are treated with kindness or severity, according to the good or bad disposition of their masters. Custom, however, has established certain rules with regard to the treatment of slaves, which it is thought dishonorable to violate. Thus the domestic slaves, or such as are born in a man's own house, are treated with more lenity than those who are purchased with money...

But these restrictions on the power of the master extend not to the care of prisoners taken in war, nor to that of slaves purchased with money. All these unfortunate beings are considered as strangers and foreigners, who have no right to the protection of the law, and may be treated with severity, or sold to a stranger, according to the pleasure of their owners."

Sometime in the 7th century, export slavery would change the nature and scope of this sordid practice, leading up to the ultimate transformation of slavery, the transatlantic slave trade.

The Trans-Saharan Slave Trade

The first few batches of slaves to be transported across the Sahara Desert were likely prisoners of war. After enduring brutal defeats by their enemies on the battlefield, men who managed to escape being shot down by arrows or stabbed by swords were strung up and shackled before being forced to meet a fate possibly worse than death.

Slavery, in any form, is no way for a person to exist. One is stripped of personhood, and generations of their offspring are often doomed to servitude. Many would eagerly choose death over slavery, except that slave-owners made even death a rare luxury. While being dragged across the hot Sahara, slaves were fed just enough to keep them alive. This was the practice among slave traders to protect their "merchandise" and by slave-owners to preserve their wealth.

King Sneferu of ancient Egypt was arguably the first to have brought captured slaves from Sudan to his kingdom, but the trans-Saharan slave trade scaled up with the activities of the Berbers, the Arabs, and their camels.

Around 650 CE, much of North Africa had been permeated by Islam. The Arabs had conquered kingdoms from Egypt to Algeria and taken over the trade routes that connected these nations to other parts of the continent. Initially, there were only two main trade routes, leading from North Africa to regions in Lake Chad and the Niger Bend. However, more trade routes were discovered by the 8th century.

Slaves became items of trade between West Africa and Muslim North Africa. Gold was also another major item of trade; it was typically exchanged for salt from North Africa. Taghaza, which was located in the North African desert region of Mali, had vast salt reserves and was an important source of salt. Slaves would mine the salt and portion it into thin slabs to sell at the Timbuktu markets, which was also part of the Mali Empire. After purchasing and exchanging their salt for gold, the Berbers could resell the gold to Arabs. This interaction encouraged the conversion of many Berbers to Islam.

As the years went by in the Early Middle Ages, the demand for slaves in the Arab Muslim Empire and the Christian Roman Empire increased. It should be mentioned that the slavers from North Africa, especially the Berbers and Arabs, typically had a slightly lighter skin color compared to the West Africans. The latter were called "blacks" by the North Africans, and the color of their skin soon became a justification for being enslaved.

Unlike gold or salt, the slave traders from North Africa did not always buy slaves. They took to raiding communities across the Sahara and capturing people for sale at slave markets. Another common tactic used, especially on children, was enticing them with sweets. The slave traders would approach gullible children, offer them treats, and trick them into following them to some undisclosed location.

Morocco, Cairo, Tripoli, and Algiers in North Africa became hubs of the slave trade. The Saharan trade routes between North Africa and West Africa became regular passages for slave caravans. A standard slave caravan had about one thousand camels, but slave traders sometimes traveled in large groups on up to twelve thousand camels. No matter how many camels a slave caravan had, no slaves were allowed to ride them. They were shackled and forced to trek the hot, sandy desert from their homelands to North Africa, where a harder life awaited them.

After arriving at their destinations, the slaves were assigned various forms of unpaid labor. Male slaves often performed hard manual labor at construction sites, farms, and mines. A few of them were castrated and made to work as palace eunuchs. Women were often put into domestic slavery or became sex slaves or concubines. The mines had the worst slavery conditions during this era. Thousands of slaves—men, women, and children—were worked to death in the salt and copper mines across North Africa. They were scarcely fed and brutally exposed to the most despicable treatment by mine officials, who would replace any slave who died in the mines with another slave.

Slaves were given as tributes or as gifts to emperors and their officials. When the Christian state of Makuria (a Nubian kingdom) was invaded by the Egyptian Muslim caliphate in the 7th century, Makuria signed a peace treaty, agreeing to supply slaves as tributes to Egypt every year. This pact held ground for at least the next six hundred years.

While North Africa ravaged West Africa in their pursuit of slaves to transport across the Sahara, another form of slavery prevailed around the Indian Ocean. The Indian Ocean is located mostly in Asia, but it links to East Africa and the Americas (via the Pacific Ocean).

The trade of African slaves along this route began with the invasion of the Swahili coast by the Muslim Arabs in the 9th century. You will recall that the Muslims began their expansionist agenda in North Africa in the 7th century and then moved to other parts of the continent. The Swahili coast was situated in East Africa, near the Indian Ocean. After the region became part of the Islamic empire, slave traders flocked to the coast to capture the natives to sell. From the coast, they advanced into the inland of what is now Tanzania, Kenya, Malawi, and Mozambique.

The Bantu people of the Swahili coast were the most targeted group. The Bantus are a collective of over one hundred ethnic groups who settled all over East Africa. In what was a mass forced exodus over the Indian Ocean, the Bantus found themselves on slave ships headed to North Africa, where they were subsequently sent to Indian islands. Like slaves from West Africa, these slaves were supplied to mines, households, and plantations.

The 15th century opened with the emergence of new slavers who were not black at all. They were from a faraway land in Europe called Portugal, and they were not the only ones who would encroach on the African continent with an insatiable demand for slaves.

The Transatlantic Slave Trade

Their destination was Point Comfort, but comfort had been the opposite of their experience on the *White Lion*, the war-commissioned ship that had brought them far away from home to a strange world.

About twenty of them survived the past hard months at sea, but more than twenty had left Angola. The disheveled, horrified, and twenty some Angolans had probably lost track of time. It was August 1619, months after they had been kidnapped from their homes in Ndongo and Kongo in Africa.

The Angolans would be sold off to new masters in the British colony of Virginia, and they would be the first of millions of Africans to be transported to the Americas over the next three centuries.

As one of the most violent crimes against humanity, the transatlantic slave trade was a major event in African history. It began with the incursion of the Portuguese into the coasts of West Africa to purchase slaves beginning in the mid-15th century. They had seen the practice during their relations with North Africans and knew how lucrative it would be to join the business. Considering that slavery had existed in the African continent for centuries before the transatlantic slave trade, the Europeans had their eyes set on purchasing slaves since their earliest contact with Africa. However, seafaring technologies in Europe had not evolved far enough yet, and no ships could endure ocean travel from Africa with that many people.

The transformations in shipbuilding came during the 15th century, enabling Europeans from other countries, such as Britain, France, Spain, and Denmark, to establish outposts on the coasts of Africa.

Medicine was not advanced enough to combat malaria and other tropical diseases at the time, so the European slave traders relied on African agents, usually native chiefs and leaders, to bring slaves from the inland to the coast. Natives were captured in raids and wars or by kidnapping, extortion, and trickery. They were then sold to the Europeans and transported far away.

The structure of the transatlantic slave trade was triangular, at least for the most part. It began with the Europeans purchasing slaves from the African elites and slave traders. In exchange for slaves, the African elites and traders were paid in textile, glass, food items, and sometimes guns. From there, the Europeans transported the purchased slaves across the Atlantic Ocean to the Americas, marking the second part of the triangle. In the Americas, slaves would be bought for a much higher price than they had been purchased. The European slave traders would then return to Europe with a wealth of tobacco, sugar, coffee, cotton, and other items. This marked the third and final part of the triangular trade system.

It took an estimated eight weeks to reach the Americas from the coasts of Africa. The average slave ship was uniquely built. The upper decks of slave ships were for the European traders and their roomy cabins. The bottom deck was where one hundred to seven hundred African captives were chained to slabs and stored as cargo. European slavers anticipated the deaths of captives while at sea, so they sought to board as many as possible on a ship.

The captives would be stacked atop one another, with no free movement. They would have been stripped, branded, and shackled on their hands and feet before being wedged into the bottom decks of the ships. The months spent at sea were abysmal. The Africans suffered from suffocation, malnutrition, and the rotten stench of filth, which led to the popular notion that a slave ship could be smelled from a distance by other ships. Diseases caused by the appalling conditions on the slave ships resulted in the deaths of many captives. Others were tortured to death by the slavers aboard or driven to the edge of committing suicide. Captives who died at sea, numbering about 1.8 million, were disposed into the Atlantic Ocean to be food for sharks, along with injured or sickly captives.

Revolts did occur during these voyages, especially starting in the 17th century. These revolts were usually quelled, and the ringleaders were almost always punished by death and torture. As a preventive measure, male captives were shackled by the neck to each other.

Slave ships were also prone to violent external attacks from pirates, who treated the captives just as inhumanely. Sexual and physical abuse were common on slave ships, and in instances of extended voyages brought on by unpredicted sea weather, food rations for captives would run out or be cut off.

The transatlantic slave trade swept the African continent. The Americas were soon populated by generational slaves whose living conditions often barely improved from the horrific forced voyages their ancestors had undertaken. Children born into slavery remained the property of their parents' owners, and they endured hard labor on plantations, factories, mines, and households.

Over twelve million Africans were captured and forcefully transported to the Americas (North America, Central America, South America, and the Caribbean) to be enslaved, which would alter the course of world history forever.

The Abolition of the Slave Trade

By the 18th century, the black race had become closely identified with slavery.

Long after the abolition of the slave trade, blacks would still be treated ignobly by the white population as lower-class humans, a long-lasting legacy that affects contemporary societies.

The clamor for the end of the slave trade began with the victims of it. Slavery had been so ingrained in the lives of the people that religious and constitutional justifications existed for it. Freedom from systemic oppression would be no easy feat, but the new generations of Africans who had been slaves their whole lives desperately sought a change.

It is important to note that slavery was a very lucrative business. In contrast to the African elites and traders who sold off their fellow natives, many European slave traders were stupendously wealthy. And the free labor of thousands of slaves in the Americas led to the accumulation of wealth for their owners. European governments directly benefited from the slave trade by taxing slave-owners or their businesses.

Slave auctions, discount sales, and promotional offers were completely legal, and slave rebellions were treated as illegal mutinies to be punished by the law or by slave-owners themselves, according to their discretion.

Centuries of this suppressed outrage soon escalated into revolts calling for the slave trade to be abolished. Meanwhile, a few other factors would make the difference between past revolts and those of the 18th century.

For instance, the continent of Europe was ushered into the Age of Enlightenment in the late 17th century. New sciences and technologies were discovered, and machines were developed to replace manual labor. Machines became cheaper, more efficient, and did not need to be fed to work. Soon, the use of slaves became increasingly considered an elaborate, more expensive means of production. While Western slave-owners benefited from the rush of intellectual and scientific evolution, they were unwilling to let go of their acquired human property. It would take years of mounting pressure and bloody slave rebellions for them to give the practice up.

The earliest abolitionists in history were slaves like Olaudah Equiano who managed to buy their freedom from their "kind" masters, and white colonists like Benjamin Lay who were motivated by their repulsion of slavery. These individuals, along with hundreds (possibly thousands) of other unnamed abolitionists, began an unstoppable movement in the late 1700s.

The Society for Effecting the Abolition of the African Slave Trade was established in 1787 in Pennsylvania. The Quakers in Georgia had emerged much earlier, and the two groups of Quakers launched anti-slavery campaigns. Some churches in Europe and the Americas held moral stances against slavery, but it was only during the Age of Enlightenment that things began to change.

Similarly, a historic anti-slavery revolution broke out in Saint-Domingue, Haiti, in 1791 against the oppressive rule of French overlords. Slaves revolted en masse against torture. They were led by a former slave named Toussaint Louverture. Fueled by their collective anger and desperation to be freed from the white slave-owners, the enslaved Haitians went on a rampage. Ex-slaves and runaway slaves joined forces with others who were still slaves to do more than poison their masters. With Toussaint Louverture at the front lines of a formidable movement, the anti-slavery force grew to include hundreds of thousands by 1793. The French government and slave-owners were threatened by this coalition, and military action was taken to contain the rebellion. This ended in a defeat for the Europeans in 1804.

The Haitian Revolution spread far beyond where it started—even to the Spanish colony of Santo Domingo (now called the Dominican Republic). The Haitian Revolution is regarded as the largest and most successful slave rebellion in history and a harbinger for the events that followed in the early years of the 19th century.

The early 1800s was when the slave trade was legally abolished in swift succession, with Denmark taking the lead in 1803. Britain followed with the Slave Trade Act of 1807 after efforts by members of Parliament like William Wilberforce to take action against institutionalized slavery. The US Congress ratified an end to the slave trade in 1808. However, the illegal slave trade continued.

For instance, in 1860, *Clotilda*, the last known slave ship, sailed from West Africa to the United States of America.

Conclusion

Racism is an offshoot of the slave trade, and it remained a part of European relations with Africa. Contrary to what must have been desperately anticipated, the end of the trans-Saharan and transatlantic was not the end of black or African oppression. After slave ships stopped docking on the coasts of Africa, colonial rule would follow—another four hundred years of economic exploitation.

Variations of the slave trade still exist in contemporary Africa. Forced labor and debt slavery are rife in Congo, and child trafficking and sex and domestic enslavement are common in parts of Ghana, Benin, Ethiopia, Chad, Togo, Nigeria, and other African countries.

Efforts by humanitarian groups and others to curtail these upsurges have had minimal effect, and the enslaved remain in hopeless captivity.

Chapter 2 – Colonization, Decolonization, and Independence

Colonization: The European Issue

Long before Africa became a hotbed of colonial rule, much of the continent existed in clusters of tribal communities. History's pages show that the peak of Africa's political subjugation was in the early 20th century; however, this story begins long before that.

The story of 20th-century European colonization in Africa begins in the 15th century. The first point of contact between Africans and Europeans was trade.

The nature of this trade diversified from one African region to another, yet European traders never journeyed to inland Africa for business. They remained on the coast, and coastal African destinations, such as Angola, Algeria, and Mozambique, soon saw a rise in European settlements.

At the time, the people of Africa did not have elaborately structured political systems. Communities were led by kings, tribal chiefs, and clan leaders. The Africans were typically not averse to having foreigners on their land as long as their ground rules for peaceful and non-invasive coexistence were adhered to.

In the years that followed, the dynamics of trade with Europeans shifted from buying items to buying human beings. The African continent was subsequently plunged into a ruthless era of forced migration, with Africans being sent to the Americas, primarily the Caribbean. A recorded ten million to twelve million Africans were captured and shipped across the Atlantic Ocean to the "New World" to be enslaved on plantations and households. The slave trade was a lucrative business for the Europeans, and more traders flocked to the coastal African regions to participate.

The early 1800s saw the end of the African slave trade in many of the countries that had been participating in it. With the decline of the slave trade, it could be expected that the Africans would no longer see as many European slavers—or any Europeans at all, save for the insufferable slave smugglers. Instead, new efforts geared at penetrating inland Africa intensified.

You may wonder why it had been so difficult for the Europeans to settle in the interior of Africa before this period. After all, the Africans were militarily ill-equipped against the Europeans and would not have been able to hold them off for too long.

First, the Africans held a territorial advantage. More importantly, they were accustomed to the tropical climate. On the other hand, Europeans had little knowledge of the landscape, and the medical technologies they had were not enough to ensure their survival in the tropics. There was also the issue of malaria, which killed one to six out of ten Europeans who managed to access inland Africa.

This inaccessibility, plus the distraction of all that money the Europeans made as slave traders, kept them contented with the coastal regions, but all that would soon change.

The Long Depression of the 1870s rocked America and Europe for over a decade. In Europe, the Long Depression was a period of economic crises, partly caused by excessive funding for long-term territorial wars.

It is important to note that European politics was dominated by competition. The quest to emerge as a world power drove major European nations, such as Britain, Germany, France, Belgium, Portugal, Russia, and Italy, to engage in constant conflicts. Each one of these countries sought economic expansion and would stop at nothing to achieve military and political domination over other nations in Europe and their colonies.

This rivalry caused a major dip in nations' coffers, and with the onset of an economic recession, the European powers desperately sought a solution.

The Forerunners

Meanwhile, back in Africa, the Africans were seeing less of slave traders and more of a new crop of Europeans. They called themselves explorers.

Unlike slavers, the explorers were not content with staying on the coast. Their curiosities lay far beyond the seaports, and they launched expeditions into the African interior, mapping out the geography of the continent and getting familiar with the native inhabitants as they made their journey.

A few notable names were David Livingstone, Henry Morton Stanley, and Carl Peters. During their adventures in Africa, they happened upon more intriguing discoveries than they could have imagined. Africa was more than what it seemed from the coast. The lands were rich with vast reserves of untapped natural resources, such as timber, gold, rubber, ivory, coal, petroleum, palm oil, and even diamonds.

To them, Africa was a literal gold mine.

Malaria and yellow fever remained threats to further expeditions until quinine, a medicine invented by French researchers, was discovered to be a cure for malaria. With this cure in hand, explorers and another group of Europeans, Christian missionaries, infiltrated the interior of Africa.

Religious missions in Africa had played a major role in calling for the abolition of the slave trade. Christian missionaries trooped into the African continent with the purpose of converting the native population from their diverse traditional beliefs (including Islam) to Christianity. This was borne out of their perceived responsibility to show the people of Africa the path of regeneration (a second birth through accepting Christ) and turn their minds toward more "legitimate" forms of trade to replace the abolished slave trade.

Initially, the Christian missionaries were met with staunch resistance from conservative Africans and the harsh climate, but they were successful in the coastal areas. This was because

European settlements on the African coast had multiplied significantly, with the area becoming their base.

When the early 19th century arrived, another influx of missions from Anglican, Methodist, Baptist, and Catholic churches were sent to Africa. The activities of white missionaries, former slaves who returned as African Christians, and mulattoes from the coast culminated in the eventual acceptance of Christianity in many parts of Africa. The construction of churches, hospitals, and institutions of Western education also attracted Africans to the Western way of thinking. While Islam successfully retained its stronghold in the northeast, other traditional religions were gradually supplanted.

Explorers and missionaries sent reports of their progress to their home countries. When they faced stiff opposition from Africans, they requested their governments to provide protection. It was only a matter of time before the discoveries of Africa kindled imperialist motivations in Europe.

The Scramble for Africa

The Mad Rush

One day in June 1878, Belgian King Leopold II received a Welsh-American explorer named Henry Morton Stanley in his stately palace in Brussels.

The king had lofty plans to carve out a slice of the African continent for himself, and Stanley was quite familiar with the region, having explored parts of it in his search for his colleague, David Livingstone.

Stanley, who had been notorious for acts of violence against the Africans he encountered while sojourning the continent, had been sidelined by the British government. His requests to be commissioned to bring Africa under British subjugation were ignored on account of his killing natives indiscriminately and looting ivory.

When Stanley was summoned by a keener Leopold II, he found a man of like mind. Leopold II had his eyes set on a jewel in the Congo Basin of Central Africa. Stanley was given authority to initiate treaty discussions with the local chiefs in Congo. Under the guise of philanthropy and "civilizing" Africa, Stanley set sail under the banner of King Leopold II to execute his assignment.

Stanley was not favorably disposed to many natives, yet his message from a "generous" king of the Belgians was well received by the chieftains. Little did they know that Leopold had more sinister plans.

Stanley's first report to King Leopold II about Congo was the prospects of rubber mining. Like gold and timber, rubber was in high demand in Europe, making it highly valuable. Congo had vast reserves of rubber, and the thought of how wealthy he'd become by owning it all must have kept Leopold II up at night.

However, Belgium lacked the finances to fund his venture. Leopold II needed international support. At the same time, he could not let on that he had a personal imperialist agenda for Congo, so he disguised his missions to Central Africa as purely philanthropic.

Other countries in Europe had their eyes on various parts of Africa, and multiple covert incursions were already underway. The network of intelligence communications between explorers in Africa and European authorities grew stronger. The ultimate desire of each nation was to control more parts of Africa than anyone else, as it meant more wealth, prestige, and political power.

In time, the French acquired intel that, contrary to his claims, Leopold was secretly moving to establish a colony in Congo. Immediately, France commissioned Pierre de Brazza, an officer of the navy, to Congo. His mission was to bring parts of Congo under French control before Leopold laid claim to the whole region. The success of this mission and the establishment of Congo Brazzaville (named after Brazza) in 1883 slightly upset Leopold II's venture, but Belgium and France were not the only players in the game.

Germany, under the leadership of Otto von Bismarck, was also on a quest for world domination. In the early 1880s, the German colonies in Africa stretched from the southwest to Cameroon and also included Tanganyika and Togoland. Britain was marking its territory in many parts of West Africa. After defeating Austria in the mid-1800s, Italy sought to expand to Eritrea, Ethiopia, and other parts of East Africa. Portugal was not left out of the scramble either, especially in parts of Congo and Guinea and some regions in southern Africa.

The fear that Germany would take over their claimed portions increased tensions between Germany and Britain, France, and Italy. War was imminent in Europe, increasing the countries' desires to exploit their colonies for economic gains. They also wished to use them as military bases.

Leopold II opined that Africa did not have to be the reason for deathly rivalries. If the colonizing countries could agree to live by certain rules of engagement, the partition of Africa could be peaceably executed. This idea eventually reached the ears of the powerful Otto von Bismarck of Germany. In 1884, he summoned thirteen European nations and the United States for a historic conference in Berlin. According to some sources, the Berlin Conference was a suggestion made by Portugal because of its desire to control a part of Congo. The proposition was made to Bismarck, and the Berlin Conference was then scheduled.

A satirical cartoon of Leopold and other imperialists portioning Africa at the Berlin Conference

The Berlin Conference was a roundtable of European nations dividing up the African continent for themselves. The representatives from these countries gathered around a map of

Africa to decide who got what without the participation of the landowners and natives. They planned to use every means necessary to seize the parts of Africa they desired.

Of course, these motives were dressed up with diplomatic terms, such as free trade with Africa. The purported aim of this trade was mutually beneficial relations with the African natives. This seems like a mostly humanitarian endeavor, but it was all a façade.

With the exception of the United States, the nations represented at the Berlin Conference legitimized their claim to Africa and went on to ruthlessly execute it. At the Berlin Conference, rival European nations found common ground and redirected their animosity toward one another to someone else.

The Berlin Conference is vital in the timeline of colonization but not as the cause of the Scramble for Africa, as some accounts erroneously put it. The scramble had already begun, and the Berlin Conference provided the European imperialists with their much-needed justification for an invasion.

The Execution

On the afternoon of Saturday, November 15th, 1884, the day the Berlin Conference kicked off, 80 percent of Africa governed themselves. Local and traditional chiefs existed as the political helmsmen in their communities, and there are accounts of a certain sultan of Zanzibar who made efforts to be invited to the Berlin Conference.

The events that followed the conference made it clear why Africans had been excluded from the "humanitarian summit." The incursion of Europeans into the African interior rose astronomically, and the traditional leaders were made to relinquish their authority to foreign overlords through subtle means. Where subtlety failed, military force was threatened and unleashed.

The Africans had barely recovered from having their families and societies utterly disrupted during the slave trade when the violent winds of imperialism came raging in.

The reality of "owning" Africa led the Europeans to discover that the continent was more geographically intricate than they had mapped out. The vast native communities, including those in proximity to one another, spoke different dialects and had diverse cultures. This posed a great challenge to the European administration.

As a solution, the Europeans embarked on the next phase of their domination: an aggressive reorganization of the political and cultural boundaries of African communities. Independent tribes and local communities were forcefully merged into larger political entities called colonies.

This arrangement was made solely for ease of colonial administration, but it was without any consideration for the social and cultural differences of the people groups who had been merged. This sent cultural shockwaves throughout the continent, yet the Africans were helpless against their captors. This was a result of the disunity of being merged with other people groups that were entirely different and the military advantage of the Europeans.

Congo, which was under the rule of Leopold II, was one of the worst hit by imperialist aggression. It was nothing like the "Free State," a term that was also prescribed to other European colonies. Congo, its inhabitants, and all its resources became the private property of King Leopold II. Hard labor in rubber mines was imposed on the native inhabitants, and they suffered painful deaths at the behest of the king if they resisted.

In parts of West Africa, the system of indirect rule was introduced by Britain. The traditional rulers were left to administer the people but only as figureheads controlled by the British government. The French also enforced a system of assimilation in West Africa. This system was aimed at making the African natives into lower-class Frenchmen. They were forced to speak, act, and dress like the French, which eliminated the need for traditional rulers. Portugal's method of colonization was similar to France's. As the first European empire to extend into Africa, Portugal held a firm monopoly on trade throughout its colonies in Central Africa.

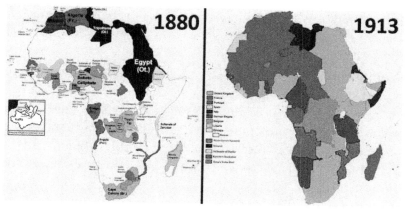

A comparison of Africa in 1880 and 1913.

Whether diplomatic or outright aggressive, the nature of European colonization in Africa was extremely exploitative. Similar to the abolished slave trade, imperialism legitimized the transportation of natural and mineral resources from Africa to Europe at the natives' expense. Artistic sculptures, monuments, and other artifacts of immense cultural importance to the Africans were also carted away.

In the seventy years after the Berlin Conference, the tables had turned. The Africans no longer held the majority control of the continent; the percentage of European-controlled regions in Africa shot up to a staggering 90 percent. While this was indicative of imperialism's tremendous success, it also highlights the existence of a few African regions that did not yield to the typhoon that swept through the continent.

But how did they evade the imperialists?

The Evaders

Ethiopia, which existed in the late 1800s as a powerful East African empire, had previously been in conflict with Italy over the colonization of Eritrea.

During the Scramble for Africa, Italy claimed Eritrea as a colony, but it would take more than Berlin Conference propaganda to remove Eritrea from Ethiopia's stronghold. Ethiopia was a formidable rival, and its emperor, Menelik II, was a powerful empire builder who would not concede to Italy's threats. This brought Ethiopia and Eritrea into a series of conflicts and years of military engagement.

You might be wondering what was so great about Eritrea. Eritrea was (and still is) a strategically located region along the coast of the Red Sea and rich in mineral resources, notably gold, copper, marble, zinc, iron ore, limestone, oil, natural gas, granite, and potash. These varied reserves were incredibly attractive to any imperialist. Ethiopia and Italy certainly had their eyes on Eritrea's vast resources.

After a protracted conflict, Emperor Menelik II of Ethiopia agreed to a compromise with the Italians. A treaty was signed in Wuchale, Ethiopia, in 1889, allowing both Italy and Ethiopia to keep parts of Eritrea to themselves without crossing the boundaries of the other.

The Treaty of Wuchale was documented in both Italian and Amharic, the latter being the official language of Ethiopia. With colonization rapidly spreading throughout Africa in the late 1800s, the Italians must have thought it a perfect time to initiate a complete takeover of Eritrea.

This resulted in another wave of conflict regarding the Amharic version of Article 17 of the Wuchale Treaty. "His Majesty the King of Kings of Ethiopia could allow you to make use of the Government of His Majesty the King of Italy for all businesses he had with other powers or government."

In the Italian version of the treaty, the phrase "could allow" was documented as "allows," implying that the ruler of Ethiopia was obligated to conduct foreign relations under the Italian government. This was equivalent to ceding his authority to the king of Italy.

Emperor Menelik II saw that this was an attempt to use trite semantics to assert dominance over Ethiopia and repealed it instantly. He was right. The Italians had resolved to take back not just all of Eritrea but the entire Ethiopian Empire.

The Italian government responded to Menelik's resistance with a military confrontation that escalated into the Battle of Adwa, which took place in March 1896.

Emperor Menelik II of Ethiopia

Menelik II's army of men and women marched out and put up an impressive front against the Italians. The Battle of Adwa ended in a decisive victory for Ethiopia. This earned the African nation the support of Russia and France. Emperor Menelik II did not push his victory further than necessary, though. What mattered to him the most was the preservation of Ethiopia's independence.

The victory at the Battle of Adwa cemented Ethiopia's status as one of the few independent African countries in 1899. Although Italy had been defeated, it would make a comeback and annex parts of Ethiopia in the 1930s. However, even that situation didn't last very long.

You will find in some historical sources that Ethiopia was excluded from colonialism because there was nothing in the region to be exploited. That is not necessarily true. Ethiopia was a landlocked region with extensive green fields for farming and agriculture. Its lack of mineral resources did not render it unattractive. Were it not for the efforts of Menelik II, the Italians would likely have made Ethiopia into a colony.

Another nation that was exempted from the widespread European domination in Africa was Liberia. Unlike Ethiopia, the unique circumstances that led to the creation of Liberia protected it from European imperialism, not its resistance.

After the abolition of the slave trade, America became home to many freed slaves who had contrasting ideas about how to go about their collective freedom. While some desired to go to Africa, others thought to stay in America and fight for a place as real citizens.

Concurrently, ideological conflicts broke out between white Americans who wanted the freed slaves out of America and others who staunchly disagreed. In 1817, the American Colonization Society was created by white men (some of them slave-owners), and their mission was to send freed slaves to Africa. Members of this society did not necessarily have humanitarian motives for this (although some did), but they backed the freed slaves who were willing to migrate.

The destination was a new settlement on the west coast, which the freed slaves reached in 1821. It became known as Liberia in 1824.

Liberia was popularized as a colony of America and home to migrant African Americans. This rendered the region off-limits to the encroaching Europeans during the Scramble for Africa. The natives who had inhabited the region were pushed back by the new settlers, and an American-type political structure was installed. Liberia gained independence from America in 1847.

On the topic of African regions that evaded European imperialism, the Dervish State is another worthy mention. The Dervish State was a coalition of clans from what is now known as Somalia. Mohammed Abdullah Hassan saw how much of Africa had been occupied by European invaders.

From his humble beginnings as a nomadic herder to his rise as a religious and political leader in the early 20th century, Hassan resolved to fight European colonialism and the propagation of Christianity in his homeland. He rallied thousands of people from his Somali hometown and other neighboring communities to resist the British imperialists. At the time, the peoples of Somaliland were also fending off Italian and Ethiopian invasions.

Hassan rose to the occasion and was at the forefront of the resistance against Christianity and the colonizers. His eloquence and charisma drove up the number of followers, attracting many from Islamic clans. In 1908, the Dervish State attacked the British forces and forced them to retreat from the Somalian inland. Hassan quickly became known among the British as "Mad Mullah." Until its collapse in 1920, the Dervish State was never colonized.

Decolonization and Independence

It had been hundreds of years since Africa was partitioned at a table of European imperialists. The reality of this partition hit the Africans the hardest.

Despite the successful import of Christianity, Western education, and other infrastructure to the "uncivilized" African continent, colonial rule represented a period of systemic oppression and discrimination against the real owners of the land.

A few communities had violently opposed the imposition of foreign rule but were subdued by superior European weaponry. However, they were not silenced forever. The colonial governments had to frequently deal with uprisings and rebellions. A good number of these anti-colonial struggles were extinguished before the mid-1900s when rebellions happened on a larger scale.

Decolonization was the eventuality of it all, but what did it really mean for those who had been affected? Obviously, decolonization was the end of colonization, but its implications went deeper than that. First, decolonization marked the beginning of a political order in Africa that was mostly modeled after the West's structure.

There was no going back to Africa's former existence as a cluster of independent communities. Attempts by certain ethnic groups to break away from the colonial-crafted political states they had been merged into were put off, often violently. For the most part, the ideology of democracy and other Western polities stayed, despite formidable efforts by anti-Western Africans to scrub away the European influences.

Before exploring the extent of this influence, the decolonization story of Africa has quite the backstory.

The Awakening

Many factors contributed to the eventual relinquishment of power by the European imperialists across Africa, but it all began with sheer exhaustion. The natives were weary of minority rule and having their lands, mineral resources, and labor exploited by foreigners. The slave trade had been a horrific experience that they'd not fully recovered from before the imperialists took over. For generations afterward, Africans had been mistreated and forcefully conscripted to join two world wars that, for the most part, had nothing to do with them.

This brings us to another factor that caused the sweep of anti-colonial ambitions throughout Africa. During the First and Second World Wars, Africans were forced to join the armies of their colonial governments. An estimated 2.5 million Africans were involved in the world wars as foot soldiers, carriers, and military camp servants. Civilians also bore the brunt of the war, especially the First World War. Despite the origins and location of the main war fronts in Europe, many offensives took place on African soil. This caused the deaths of many civilian and African soldiers. In the Second World War, Africans were transported to war fronts in Europe, where they experienced that death knew no color. The enforced notion that their colonial masters were invincible washed away on the battlefield when they saw white soldiers turning on and killing one another.

After the Second World War, the African veterans returned home, traumatized by the war yet emboldened by political awareness. This was similar to the educated African elites' experience. Few Africans were fortunate enough to travel out of their home countries to Europe for formal education during the colonial period. Their exposure sparked nationalist motivations.

The Atlantic Charter of 1941 provided the justification for the African nationalists' demand for independence. The charter was drawn up during the Second World War and was a statement by the United States and the United Kingdom on their goals for the post-war era. At the time of its making, the Atlantic Charter sought to restore peace and stability to the war-torn world. An important part of this charter was the agreement to allow all peoples to decide their sovereignty and ultimately restore their rights to self-government.

When the independence struggles heightened in the 1950s, US President Franklin Delano Roosevelt reminded the British government of the Atlantic Charter. Reluctant to let go of their colonies, the British government argued that by "all peoples," they referred to only European states. In response, the United States insisted that the clause applied to all people, including Africans.

In 1960, the United Nations General Assembly put out a "Declaration on the Granting of Independence to Colonial Countries and Peoples." This was a major boost to the African nationalists' morale, and from there, the timeline of African liberation increased to full speed.

Winners, Losers

The African independence wave of the 1950s began in Libya when the United Kingdom of Libya declared King Idris was its constitutional leader. The country had been annexed into the British and French empires after the defeat of Italy in the Second World War. Despite the breakaway from colonial rule, King Idris was famed for his cordial alliance with the United Kingdom and the United States. This remained the norm until famous anti-Western political revolutionary Muammar al-Gaddafi overthrew the Libyan government and founded a new order. Gaddafi would contribute to the liberation of many other African countries in the years to come.

In 1956, Sudan, Tunisia, and Morocco joined the league of independent African nations. Parts of these countries had been partitioned and colonized by Britain, France, and Spain for most of the late 1800s and early 1900s. The Republic of Guinea was next, gaining independence in October 1958.

The 1960s was the peak decade of Africa's decolonization. In 1960 alone, a total of seventeen African countries were liberated from colonial rule, such as Nigeria, Senegal, Togo, Somalia, Niger, Burkina Faso, Mali, Congo, Cameroon, Ivory Coast, Mauritania, and Gabon. These events prompted the UN to declare the decolonization of all African colonies in December 1960, encouraging the rapid independence of other regions.

Burundi, Algeria, and Rwanda became independent from Belgium and France in 1962, while Britain lost at least nine more colonies in the mid- to late 1960s. The timeline of independence blazed on into the 1970s, and on April 18th, 1980, the British colony of Rhodesia (modern-day Zimbabwe) gained independence.

For the European colonizers, the decolonization era signified a significant loss of their direct control over the African continent. While they had been preoccupied as belligerents during the First and Second World Wars, their colonies had erupted in more aggressive rebellions by determined natives. The involvement of Africans in the world wars and the exposure of a few to Western education gave African nationalism more impetus.

As you will later discover, European nations that had lost either world war had to relinquish their colonies to the winners. This reshuffling added another layer of colonialism in Africa. It was bad enough that their lands had been reduced to being the property of a country in Europe. But being tossed around from owner to owner and the rude shock of adjusting to a new colonial authority as spoils of war was more than they could take, fueling resentment.

Although much of Africa was officially independent of colonist powers by the late 1900s, the former colonial authorities had not completely vanished from the continent. In fact, there still exists the notion of neocolonialism. This idea is that Africa has never truly been free from colonialism and that rather than independence, what truly transpired in the mid- to late 1900s was a transition to dependency. This possibly rings true in light of the constant interference of ex-colonizers in events of post-independent Africa.

Outside nations have become involved in African elections, funded civil war belligerents, and maintained military bases in their ex-colonies. We will explore this topic later, but suffice it to say that it is debatable as to whether or not Africa was ever truly liberated.

Chapter 3 – Africa and the World Wars

The First World War

For this story, we go back to the early 1900s, when much of Africa had been claimed by European imperialists. You will recall that the Scramble for Africa happened as a result of the desire of nearly every European nation to emerge as the most powerful, both politically and economically. You will also recall that Europe itself had been a theater of conflict and political rivalry before the discovery of Africa.

Well, the year was 1914, and a certain Austrian archduke, Franz Ferdinand, and his wife were being chauffeured in his convertible car along a small road in Sarajevo, Bosnia. A nineteen-year-old Bosnian Serb appeared out of a nearby café and fired two shots from his pocket-sized pistol at the archduke and his wife, killing them almost instantly.

Archduke of Austria-Hungary and his wife in Sarajevo

The death of Archduke Franz Ferdinand, the heir to the Austro-Hungarian throne, and his wife Sophie was a prelude to the First World War, also known as the Great War. Austria-Hungary received the news of the archduke's death. It ultimately declared war on Serbia. Austria-Hungary had been itching for a war with Serbia, and Franz Ferdinand's death gave it the perfect pretext for declaring war.

Serbia enlisted the help of Russia, France, and Britain against Austria-Hungary, Germany, and the Ottoman Empire. The Serbs' allies became known as the Allied forces (or the Entente), and Austro-Hungary's allies were named the Central Powers.

The First World War began on July 28th, 1914, and multiple offensives were launched by both sides at various locations, including their respective colonies in Africa.

North Africa

In the ugly wake of a world war, strategies were the order of the day. Beyond direct assaults and open offensives, both the Central Powers and the Allies developed and executed many campaigns to weaken the opposition.

African colonies were extensions of political and economic power in Europe. Consequently, African colonies became targets. In 1914, Germany and the Ottoman Empire hatched a plot to incite uprisings in British colonies.

The target was narrowed to the British-controlled parts of the Egyptian coast, and a certain Islamic religious order known as the Senussi seemed perfect for the job. The Senussi was an Islamic group originating from parts of Egypt and Libya. In the not-so-distant past, this group had pushed back Italy's colonial attempts and remained independent for the years that followed.

Although a Muslim order, the Senussi had no enmity with the British colonialists, even though the latter had already taken over parts of coastal Egypt and annexed them into the British Empire. Aware of the relationship between the British and the Senussi, the Central Powers were convinced that all it would take to muddy the waters was a slight push.

The Central Powers' goal was to use the Senussi to set off insurrectionist campaigns in Egypt to divert British troops from the Suez Canal. The Suez Canal was an important sea trade route in Egypt, and it was under Britain's control at the time. If the British troops that occupied the coastal areas along the Suez Canal were removed, the Central Powers would gain the upper hand.

In the summer of 1915, the supreme leader of the Senussi, Ahmed Sharif as-Senussi (also known as the Grand Senussi), was approached by the Germans and Turks to consider mobilizing the repressed Muslims in Egypt for a jihad. They also appealed to the Grand Senussi's anti-colonial beliefs and indicated that Christians (the British) were oppressing his fellow Muslims.

The Grand Senussi was reluctant to give in to the Central Powers, even after being supplied with troops, machine guns, artillery, and funds for the war. Later that year, the Grand Senussi was driven to action. The British learned of his calls for a jihad and dispersed forces to some of the Egyptian colonies.

The Senussi campaign, which lasted from November 1915 to February 1917, targeted the British-occupied coastal areas in Egypt, especially Sollum, Baqbaq, Barani, and Sidi. The British retreated after the first batch of sporadic attacks on coastal military bases, but they did not stay away for long.

On December 25th, 1915, a Senussi camp was infiltrated and raided by the British army, resulting in a decisive British victory. It was followed up by a string of victories, allowing them to reclaim their lost bases. With the alliance of the Senussis' old enemy, the Italians, the two-year Senussi campaign ended in victory for Britain and Italy. By 1917, the Senussi belligerents had been removed from the coasts of Egypt and forced to flee to the deserts. A peace treaty on April 12th, 1917, put an end to the hostilities.

The plans of Germany and the Ottoman Empire did not go exactly as planned. Similarly, the disruptive German invasion of Portuguese Angola in 1915 ended in victory for Portugal after many offensive campaigns. Through it all, Africans in the warring regions were forcefully conscripted to fight on the side of their colonial government. Hundreds of thousands of native casualties were recorded.

East Africa

When World War I broke out, the colonial governments in Africa initially committed to non-aggression against rival imperialists on African soil. This was because it was important to keep the "peace," which meant the continued collective repression of the African natives. This commitment had been officially sealed in the Congo Act of 1885.

In time, however, Africa became a theater for multiple campaigns in what was mostly a European war. The colonial governments spared no man or resource in the war. East Africa, an often-forgotten theater of the First World War, was a hotbed of multiple guerilla actions and daunting marches across dense jungles, arid deserts, and mountainous terrain at the expense of poorly fed and under-clothed Africans.

In August 1914, a general in the German Imperial Army named Paul von Lettow-Vorbeck devised a strategy to keep as many Allied troops away from the Western Front, which was one of the main theaters of the First World War. To do this, he planned to divert as many Allied troops to Africa as possible and keep them engaged for as long as he could.

The German colonies in East Africa included Rwanda, Burundi, and parts of Mozambique and Tanzania. Despite the orders of the governor of German East Africa to remain neutral in the war,

Lettow-Vorbeck set out on his elaborate campaign with his troops, some 300 Europeans and 2,500 Africans. While it had only taken the eloquent words of Lettow-Vorbeck to persuade some of the natives to join the German Army, Lettow-Vorbeck's mission would only be half-achieved at the expense of their untold suffering and hardship.

Meanwhile, Britain had always had concerns about Germany's unbridled ambitions to acquire more colonies. In response to Lettow-Vorbeck's big move, the British mustered over 100,000 men to face Germany's 25,000 soldiers.

Belgium and Portugal, which had been keen on staying out of the hostilities and protecting their colonies, could no longer ignore the German threat. Collectively, they rallied forty thousand troops to join the British army. The nature of the East African campaign was possibly worse than an open static affront. The Germans enlisted an estimated 350,000 African men, women, and children as carriers during the campaign. These carriers were tasked with moving heavy war machinery, weapons, and ammunitions across arduous mountainous and riverine terrains that the motor vehicles and pack animals could not cross easily. The carriers walked many miles in the scorching sun and in the rain. They traveled through jungles where wild animals posed a great threat. These duties were carried out with no pay, flimsy food rations, and no medicine if they got sick.

After a handful of initial victories, Lettow-Vorbeck's big plan to distract a large column of British troops was only partly successful. It seemed as if the British never seemed to run out of troops, forcing Lettow-Vorbeck to embrace guerilla tactics. In late 1914, the Germans raided British military positions in northern Rhodesia (now known as Zambia) and Kenya. The East African campaign became a stalemate as the months rolled by. The territories were recovered in 1916 when British General Jan Smuts led troops from South Africa to remove the Germans. The Allied troops closed in on the Germans, bolstered by columns from the Belgian Congo.

In December 1916, Lettow-Vorbeck's troops split into even smaller groups and set off on guerilla campaigns in the southern regions of German East Africa. The divisions' aim was not to be put down all at once by the enemy troops. Soon, though, one of the groups was captured and forced to surrender. By that point, the German troops were running low on food, medicine, and other supplies. A few of Lettow-Vorbeck's men began to desert or surrender, but Lettow-Vorbeck did not surrender until the end of the First World War.

Lettow-Vorbeck surrendered on November 25th, 1918, after he heard of the armistice, which had taken place fourteen days earlier. The armistice was Germany's agreement with the Allied Forces to cease all hostilities.

The war was over, but not without disastrous consequences on Africans, military personnel, and civilians alike. The tax increments on natives to fund the war and the land and food requisitions plunged them into famine. The disruption of their communal lives by forced conscription into a "white man's war" would take a long time to recover from.

An estimated 200,000 East African men, women, and children lost their lives in the campaign, and thousands more perished from famine, drought, and diseases. On top of this, the Africans' labor went unappreciated and unrewarded by the colonial authorities.

West Africa

Since France and Britain were the major colonizing powers in the West African region, they decided to jointly attack the German colonies of Togo and Cameroon in 1914. These two colonies were of tremendous strategic and economic importance to Germany, and the Allied Powers plotted to seize them from Germany's control.

On hearing their plans, the German West African government sought a truce by calling for negotiations. Efforts to get the Allied forces on board were unsuccessful, and the reality of an offensive dawned on Germany. The three colonial powers turned on the natives of their colonies, bringing about a frenzy of haphazard military recruitments.

In French West Africa, the news spread among the natives that the colonial government was recruiting African men to fight in a war that had nothing to do with them. They also learned that the poorly equipped African men were being used as fodder at the war front, where they were killed like flies. A good number of men who thought themselves likely targets of this recruitment campaign fled their homes to neighboring colonies. This wave of escape became rampant in Ivory Coast, Dahomey, and Guinea.

The desperate French ruthlessly sacked communities in their colonies, kidnapping African men or blackmailing them by imprisoning their family members. Local chiefs who stood against being used to coerce their people into joining the French Army suffered diverse forms of consequences, the least of all being imprisonment. Some had their farmsteads and livestock destroyed by French colonial authorities, and others were deposed and tortured. Compliant chiefs who met recruitment targets were rewarded with money.

Meanwhile, British West Africa set up two military regiments: the West African Frontier Force (WAFF) and the West African Regiment in Sierra Leone. The British colonies of Ghana, Sierra Leone, Gambia, and Nigeria all supplied African men for the war effort. The WAFF, for instance, had about 8,000 men at the beginning of the campaign, with more than 7,500 of them being Africans. In Ghana (then called the Gold Coast), recruitments recorded little success, with many African men deserting before they could be forced to join the army. Nigerians and Sierra Leoneans were not so lucky. Local chiefs were threatened to supply men from their communities, and young men were coerced to marry just so they could be eligible to be drafted into the war.

British West Africa eventually launched its campaign against German West Africa, combining its force with seventy thousand WAFF soldiers. These included an overwhelming majority of Nigerian men, with most of them being forcefully conscripted.

The French colonial authorities lost the most men in the skirmishes against Germany. Fifty thousand African men were lost by 1918, and sixty-three thousand new African recruits were deployed to battlefronts in Cameroon and Togo.

Despite the lack of knowledge about the terrain and the extreme climatic conditions, the campaigns in Togo and Cameroon ended in an Allied victory. The African soldiers were instrumental in navigating the dense forests and bushes. They also were used for cheap labor by the colonial governments they represented.

The Second World War

The Second World War saw the Allies (Britain, United States, China, and the Soviet Union) face off against the Axis (Germany, Italy, and Japan).

Africa was once again dragged into the conflict at the cost of over a million natives who served in diverse capacities. Volunteering was the advertised method of recruitment, but the natives knew better than to be fooled by that again. They feared they would be carted away to war fronts in Europe and that certain regions in Africa would suffer again as theaters of a foreign war.

The background of the Second World War, though multi-faceted, was not very different from the First World War. They both occurred because imperialist nations sought to expand territories and emerge as the most powerful country in the world.

After suffering defeat in the First World War, Germany lost many of its colonies to the Allied nations. In addition to this concession, Germany was compelled to accept peace at its own expense at the Paris Peace Conference in 1919, where the victorious Allies dictated the terms of the agreement. During this conference, the Treaty of Versailles was imposed on Germany, sealing the transfer of its former African colonies to the Allied forces for redistribution. Other sanctions were imposed as well. For instance, Germany had to demobilize its army and take responsibility for the damages caused by the war by paying an estimated five billion dollars to the Allies.

Subsequently, Germany did not fully follow the agreement.

In 1933, under Adolf Hitler, Germany removed itself from all obligations. Rather than align with the terms of the Treaty of Versailles, Nazi Germany embarked on a radical quest for world domination. The German invasion of Poland in September 1939 triggered another dark era of war in Europe.

The Suez Issue

The Suez Canal had always been of tremendous strategic importance to the imperial powers. It was a constructed waterway that allowed for the seamless and quick transportation of trade items, notably oil from the oilfields in Africa, to Europe without having to navigate the difficult inland.

When the Second World War broke out in 1939, the Suez Canal was under the control of the British government. Despite Egypt's independence from the British Empire, British troops still occupied the Suez Canal to protect Britain's interests. Thus, the Suez Canal quickly became a target of the Axis Powers. The series of battles that ensued were collectively named the Western Desert (or North African) campaign.

It began when the Axis forces invaded Egypt from Libya in 1940 after Benito Mussolini, Italy's dictator, declared war on Britain.

Britain had earlier attacked a fort named Capuzzo in an Italian colony of Libya, and the Italians responded with a counter-offensive three months after. Egypt and Libya would be hot zones of bombings, gunshots, and explosions.

After the Italians captured Sidi Barrani, Egypt, during the counter-offensive of September 1940, the British troops counterattacked by raiding an Italian camp in Nibeiwa, Egypt. This was the first engagement in Operation Compass.

The British enjoyed an extensive victory streak in subsequent offensives against Italy in Operation Compass. They advanced into Libya, pushing back the Italian troops. The aim was to remove both Italy and Germany from North Africa, where they posed a threat to the British control over the Suez Canal.

Defeated and exhausted, the Italians were on the brink of losing the North African campaign in 1941. The tides turned when Germany sent reinforcements called the Afrika Korps. This contingent was led by a remarkable German commander who went by the name Erwin Rommel.

Rommel had a reputation in the army for being a brilliant war strategist and fearless combatant. He had risen up the ranks in the German military and served in Hitler's personal security detail. His arrival in Libya coincided with the period when the victory-drunk British had diverted their troops from North Africa to the war front in Greece.

With Rommel on board, the German and Italian troops began a counter-advance against the British in March 1941. A blazing trail of victories for the Axis forces followed, mainly due to Rommel's extraordinary leadership. He quickly earned the alias "Desert Fox" because of his bold, almost reckless offensives in the most difficult terrains of North Africa's deserts.

Even when the terrain encumbered the supply of food and weapons to the German troops, Rommel led bloody charges against the British and pursued them back to Sollum, located on the Egyptian-Libyan border. However, the Germans and Rommel ran out of victories in August 1942 when Bernard Law Montgomery was appointed by the British government as the commander of the British army.

Montgomery led the British troops to victory in the Second Battle of El Alamein in October 1942. An estimated thirty thousand Axis soldiers were captured as prisoners of war. The Allied troops' morale was revived by this bout, and in the final lap of the campaign, the Allied forces won.

Operation Torch, as it was called, sealed the victory of the Allied forces. The United States sent in troops to fight with the British army in simultaneous offensives in Libya and parts of French North Africa.

The victory of the Allied forces in Operation Torch removed the Italian and German threats to the Suez Canal and gave new hope of victory in the ensuing campaigns of the Second World War.

Conclusion

The armies of every war front in Africa and some parts of Europe in the Second World War were fed by conscription. As traumatic and disruptive as the First World War had been, the colonial authorities proceeded to recruit and impose hard labor on Africans for the second round of fighting. Worse still, the recruited Africans who sacrificed their lives in the First and Second World Wars were ill-treated in military camps.

Despite fighting for the colonial authorities, white soldiers treated the black soldiers with racist contempt. Their food rations were different, their uniforms and weapons were of poorer quality, and, in some instances, African soldiers were not allowed to march alongside the white soldiers.

In the campaigns on African soil, the Europeans would lead the African troops through dense forests and jungles instead of regular routes to discourage the Africans from deserting. Those carted away to Europe could not easily escape from the battlefield since they were in an unknown land.

The deaths of the millions of African soldiers, carriers, camp servants, and armor bearers in the First and Second World Wars still remain largely unrecognized.

Chapter 4 – Civil War and Genocide

One of the themes of the mid-1900s was the trend of European colonies gaining independence from their overlords. After scaling through the exploitative era of colonial rule, African elites and intellectuals began to organize into groups to demand independence.

Unfortunately, their independence did not mark the beginning of the utopian existence that many had envisioned. If you recall, it was emphasized in the last chapter that during the partitioning of Africa, the colonialists restructured geopolitical communities by merging them together for ease of administration. However, there was no consideration for ethnic and/or tribal differences. These differences would continue long after the independence of former colonies, and an array of bloody civil wars would erupt among the groups that had been forced to exist as one.

The Nigerian Civil War (1967–1970)

The Onset

When Frederick Lugard purportedly "woke up, had a cup of tea, and decided to merge the Northern and Southern Protectorates of Nigeria into one," the differences between the many ethnic groups in the protectorates and their cultural incompatibilities were the least of his concerns. He had been commissioned as the colonial administrator of the region by the British government, and his job was to coordinate the affairs of the vast area as one.

Nigeria was born after Lugard's merger (or amalgamation) in 1914, and three major ethnic groups found themselves within the same country: the Hausa-Fulani, the Igbo, and the Yoruba. Other smaller groups existed as part of New Nigeria, but these three were the largest. The Igbo and the Yoruba were part of southern Nigeria, and the Hausa-Fulani held the North. Later, the South was subdivided into the southwest for the Yoruba and the southeast for the Igbo.

The consequences of Lugard's decision were initially lost on the African natives. They had found their lives utterly disrupted during the slave trade era, so the era of colonialism seemed softer. In time, however, the inherent disharmony that had existed among them long before they were forced to coexist began to rear its ugly head.

Nigeria gained independence from Britain on October 1ˢᵗ, 1960, due to the united front across all ethnic groups to rid their land of imperialists. However, only seven years into Nigeria's independence, ethnic tensions broke out again.

The first president of Nigeria was Nnamdi Azikiwe. He administered the country with Prime Minister Tafawa Balewa. On the morning of January 15ᵗʰ, 1966, a bloody coup rocked the Nigerian political scene and replaced the civilian government with a military regime.

The January 1966 coup was executed by five majors of the Nigerian Army, and it resulted in the deaths of Prime Minister Tafawa Balewa, the Premier of Northern Nigeria Ahmadu Bello, the Premier of Southern Nigeria Ladoke Akintola, and Finance Minister Festus Okotie-Eboh. President Nnamdi Azikiwe was out of the country on official business at the time and thus escaped the coup.

The motivation for the coup, as given by the plotters, was the corruption of the Nigerian government and the flamboyant lifestyles of key officials, which came at the expense of the masses. However, the coup plotters were all Igbo men, and their justification was rejected by the other ethnic tribes as a façade for their tribalist intentions. The coup's casualties were mostly Hausas and Yorubas, and to others, it seemed odd that President Azikiwe, an Igbo man, had been excluded from the violence. Yes, the president was out of the country on official business when the coup was executed, but it remains widely debated whether or not he had been tipped off beforehand.

The timing of the coup, its targeted casualties, and the emergence of Major General Johnson Aguiyi-Ironsi (also an Igbo man) as the new head of state after the coup made the Hausa-Fulani and Yorubas even more suspicious. In July 1966, a counter-coup was led by Colonel Murtala Mohammed. It knocked Aguiyi-Ironsi off the seat of power, with General Yakubu Gowon stepping up to replace him. This murderous counter-coup was a response to the January coup and an affront to the Igbos. Other motivations were the rumors of the Igbos' domination of the Nigerian Army and General Aguiyi-Ironsi's display of ethnic bigotry by refusing to persecute the January coup plotters.

Apart from the political instability caused by the counter-coup, the new military government marked a period of increased attacks on the Igbo population. Northerners described them as "vermin" and "dogs to be killed," and they formed anti-Igbo pogroms. The Igbos who lived in northern Nigeria were exterminated, and the few who escaped to other parts of the country were not safe either.

The death toll of Igbo civilians and military men rose to thirty thousand by September 1966. On one historic day in 1967, the Igbos rallied behind one man to declare an independent nation.

The Civil War

"Having mandated me to proclaim on your behalf, and in your name, that Eastern Nigeria be a sovereign independent Republic, now, therefore I, Lieutenant Colonel Chukwuemeka Odumegwu-Ojukwu, Military Governor of Eastern Nigeria, by the authority, and pursuant to the principles recited above, do hereby solemnly proclaim that the territory and region known as and called Eastern Nigeria together with her continental shelf and territorial waters, shall, henceforth, be an independent sovereign state of the name and title of The Republic of Biafra."

This announcement made by Lieutenant Colonel Ojukwu on May 30th, 1967, was the climax of the year-long ill-treatment and genocidal attacks on the Igbos. Prior to the decision to secede from Nigeria, the Igbos, represented by their governor, Chukwuemeka

Ojukwu, had attempted negotiations with the government led by Yakubu Gowon.

One notable diplomatic endeavor was the Aburi Accord of January 1967, where the Nigerian government agreed to operate the country as a loose confederation. This meant that each state in the country could hold sovereignty without the federal government's interference. However, after the meeting, the Nigerian government delayed in making good on the resolution.

Instead, Yakubu Gowon moved to break Nigeria into twelve states, further isolating the Igbos from other eastern regions. This was interpreted by Ojukwu and his people as a deliberate attempt to limit their control over their oil-rich neighbors in the east and a breach of the Aburi Accord.

The break-up of the Nigerian states.

The Nigerian federal government received the news of an independent Igbo state, Biafra, and immediately swung into action to curtail the secession. First, all supply shipments to Biafra were banned, and an offensive was launched against the Igbos.

After making the first move in what became a full-blown war, the Nigerian government solicited and acquired international support. The Biafrans were short on weapons and ammunition, but that quickly became the least of their problems. The Nigerian government blocked off their access to food and oil, which could have been used to generate funds for the war, thus putting the Biafrans at an early disadvantage.

The Nigerian government was convinced that with the proactive steps that had been taken, the war would fizzle out just as abruptly as it had begun. The Igbos took Nigeria and the world by surprise when they looked to foreign countries for support instead of surrendering. While the United Kingdom, the Soviet Union, and a host of powerful African countries openly stood with Nigeria against Biafra, China, West Germany, Spain, Portugal, France, and other African countries lent arms and alleged support to Biafra. The United States took a neutral stance that many interpreted to be support for Nigeria.

The Nigerian Civil War progressed with offensives and counter-offensives, resulting in heavy casualties on both sides. One year after the war began, the Nigerian government changed strategies. After a final offensive in June 1968, the government blocked every port and cordoned off the routes leading to inland Biafra. The civilian population of Biafra began to suffer from hunger and starvation.

This was an arguably unethical war strategy, but the Nigerian government was not stopped. Thousands of Igbos died due to extreme famine and frequent genocidal raids by the Nigerian Army. Women were ruthlessly raped and killed. Children were not spared from the violence.

Humanitarian aid was raised by concerned groups and missionary societies. Relief packages were sent to Biafra via airlift, but these often did not reach their designations. Several criticisms were made against the Nigerian government due to its violation of human rights, but this did not affect the strength of Nigeria's international support system. As a final resort, Biafra enlisted mercenaries to finish off the war, and the Nigerian government followed suit to strengthen the Nigerian troops.

With the surging death toll caused by hunger and starvation-induced diseases in Biafra, the war could only drag on for so long. Thousands of Igbos died or were murdered every day, and Biafra had expended high costs to fund the war. On January 15th, 1970, the Nigerian Civil War ended with a victory for Nigeria and the dissolution of the Republic of Biafra. Lieutenant Colonel Ojukwu and his associates fled to Cote d'Ivoire (Ivory Coast), and Biafra was reintegrated into Nigeria.

The Nigerian Civil War has been labeled as genocide, considering that unarmed Igbo civilians were the most targeted. This atrocity against men, women, and children remains unaccounted for, despite its unfolding in the full glare of the world. The Nigerian government has not issued a formal apology, and no one has been punished for the murders.

Historically, the Nigerian Civil War is a prominent event in African history since it involved the most populated country on the continent.

Somalia vs. Ethiopia

The Origins

The tensions between Somalia and Ethiopia originated in the late 1940s due to ethnic and religious conflicts. The two countries had been neighbors since the 5th century but were not very friendly toward each other. There was always conflict over which country owned one borderland and other issues.

After the unification of British Somaliland and the former Italian Somaliland to form the Somalia Republic in 1960, Ethiopia did not seem ready to let go of the part of Somaliland in its empire. Revolts broke out against the Ethiopian Empire by Somalis who wanted to join the newly independent Somalia.

Ethiopia had never felt like home to the Somalis. Not only had Christianity been imposed on them for generations, but the Ethiopian culture was also a far cry from their acceptable norms. They had been annexed into Ethiopia during the scourge of colonial rule, but with the declaration of the Somalia Republic, the

Somalis in Ethiopia protested for freedom.

The emperor of Ethiopia at the time, Haile Selassie, blatantly refused to let go of the Somali region in his empire. Particularly in Ogaden, insurrections rose against the Ethiopian government, and the emperor ordered violent repressions of the rebellion. This response only stoked the flames of conflict. The newly emerged Somali government was provoked by the ill-treatment of their fellow Somalis in Ethiopia and mustered their limited resources to challenge the Ethiopian government.

War and Aftermath

In February 1964, the troops of the Somalia Republic marched against Ethiopia and raided police posts in some strategic border towns. The overwhelming response of the Ethiopian government, which sent armored tanks, aircraft, artillery, and infantry, forced the Somali forces to retreat two months later.

This brief war is known as the Ethiopian-Somali Border War of 1964, and it was the first of many.

The Ogaden War broke out thirteen years later. This time, the sides would have the support of multiple belligerents, including the United States and the Soviet Union. Before the Ogaden War broke out in 1977, the Soviet Union switched allegiance. Prior to the war, the Soviet Union had supported Somalia as a unified republic, while Ethiopia's history of relations with Britain allowed for a cordial relationship.

As Ethiopia grappled with internal rebellions in the 1970s (an unavoidable pattern in empire-building), Somalia replenished its depleted reserves. Somalis in Ogaden wanted nothing more than a complete breakaway from Ethiopia, but things were not so simple.

The British had practically handed Ogaden over to Ethiopia in the 1940s without regard for the cultural and religious imposition that the Somalis in Ogaden were bound to suffer. The disgruntled Somalis in Ogaden must have been hopeful when the Ethiopian emperor was overthrown by the Derg, a military council. The Derg was embroiled in an internal conflict over who should take the emperor's seat, and it was only a matter of time before pockets of rebellion by other groups rose up, doing so between 1974 and 1975.

A pro-Somalian faction called the Western Somali Liberation Front jumped to the front lines of the rebellion, taking advantage of the situation in Ethiopia caused by the void in leadership. Meanwhile, in the wake of 1977, the Derg coalition produced a new Ethiopian political system led by the head of state, Mengistu Haile Mariam. It would replace the imperial monarchy.

When the news broke that Somalia was planning a more coordinated attack on Ethiopia, the Soviet Union contacted President Siad Barre of Somalia and suggested more diplomatic solutions to the conflict. However, Somalia was keen on removing Ogaden and other Somali regions from Ethiopian control.

The Soviet Union took offense at being ignored by Somalia and withdrew all support, redirecting it to Ethiopia instead. Communist nations like Cuba, North Korea, Germany, South Yemen, and Cuba also aligned with Ethiopia. China, a rival of the Soviet Union, threw its weight behind Somalia, and so did the United States, which was in the Cold War with the Soviet Union at the time. Supporting nations donated troops, funds, and other military resources to their favored side.

The first offense against Ethiopia took place in July 1977. It was a victory for Somalia, but it would be one of their last. Ethiopia's superior war arsenal and its constant wave of air attacks on Somalia decimated the latter's military resources.

The war ended with the final onslaught that inflicted thousands of Somalian casualties and forced President Siad Barre to order a retreat. The Ethiopian and Cuban forces rained havoc on the Somali forces and decimated the civilian population in a series of killings, poisoning, and rape.

The many pro-Somalian liberation groups were disintegrated. Refugees flocked to Somalia from Ogaden after the war, causing President Barre to have a new dilemma on his hands. Having exhausted Somalia's resources during the war, Somalia became heavily dependent on foreign aid. Despite the dire situation, Barre allocated a chunk of the country's resources to the teeming population of Ogaden refugees. This upset the native clans of Somalia, who spoke out against Barre's favoritism.

Eventually, the refugees became unruly. Somalia would erupt in a long-term civil war in the early 1990s. Prior to that, in 1982, another border war with Ethiopia took place, with Ethiopia leading fifteen thousand men on the offensive. Although the fifty thousand Somali troops outnumbered them by a wide margin, they were ill-equipped and attacked by surprise.

The Somali troops stood no chance against Ethiopia's T-55 tanks and MIG fighters, but the Ethiopians were not the last straw. The 1991 Somali Civil War was what cost Barre his army and his seat as the head of state. Ethiopia was effectively sidelined in the conflict, and the Somali Civil War took center stage, protracting for decades. As of this writing, the civil war is still ongoing.

The Civil Wars of Chad, Angola, and Ivory Coast

Typically, civil wars begin due to immense dissatisfaction with the government. Certain groups act out to express their animosity, which eventually escalate into large-scale wars that cause thousands and, in some cases, millions of deaths.

Uprisings had happened in nearly every part of Africa by the mid-1900s, and the most disadvantaged of all were the civilians who were essentially reduced to being spoils of war.

In this segment, the Chadian Civil War has the first spotlight. A total of four civil wars engulfed this north-central African country, the last of which continues as of this writing.

Chad's Civil War

The first Chadian Civil War was in 1965, shortly after the country gained independence from French colonial rule in August 1960.

After France's relinquishment of political power, a Chadian man of Sara descent named François Tombalbaye became the first president of independent Chad. Years before his appointment, Tombalbaye was a teacher under French colonial rule. Later, he joined partisan politics as a trade unionist. He toppled Gabriel Lisette as the leader of the Chadian Progressive Party and became the president of Chad during the country's transition to independence.

Before going into the details of Tombalbaye's presidency, it is imperative to understand the structure of Chad upon its independence. Like other African countries, Chad was created by merging diverse ethnic groups in north-central Africa, Christians and Muslims alike, for the ease of colonial administration. Following the independence struggle, the country had the Muslim North and the Christian South.

During Tombalbaye's candidacy, he enlisted the support of progressives in the South and North, excluding the more radical Islamic factions. However, in the years that followed, Tombalbaye embarked on a radical dictatorial streak that cut off his supporters in the North and even the South. His next targets were opposition parties. Tombalbaye dissolved all other political parties and declared Chad a one-party political system. He also eliminated the National Assembly and purged the civil service of all opponents. To fund his autocratic administration, Tombalbaye imposed heavy taxes on the people of Chad while being flagrant in his displays of exuberance.

The oppressed people of Chad began to protest against François Tombalbaye's government, which led to the formation of the National Liberation Front of Chad, or FROLINAT for short. This group declared war on Tombalbaye's administration, and the civil war in Chad began. FROLINAT recruited soldiers in droves and had them trained in North Korea for the war.

Members of FROLINAT rebelled through strike actions, open assaults, and assassination plots targeted at government officials. Libya lent military aid to FROLINAT, especially when Muammar Gaddafi rose to power. In 1968, Tombalbaye sought the assistance of France to quell the growing rebellion. This was in line with a mutual defense pact that France had with Chad since it was a former colony. France had agreed to lend military assistance whenever it was requested. France's intervention culminated in the death of Ibrahim Abacha, one of the key leaders of FROLINAT.

The Chadian government defeated the rebels in the battles that followed, but the rebels did not relent. When Tombalbaye ran unopposed in the 1969 presidential election, the rebels were even more inclined to use violence. The rural areas and countryside of Chad became rebel strongholds, and the Chadian Army could not penetrate them.

Despite France's continued support in tackling the rebels, Tombalbaye's administration began to fall apart shortly after his reelection. He had lost the trust of the progressive groups who had made his rise to power seamless. Worst still, the citizens loathed him for his repressive policies.

By 1972, the Chadian coffers that Tombalbaye had used to fund his elaborate government were nearly empty. He desperately sought aid from Libya, which had supported FROLINAT at the onset of the war. His relations with Libyan terrorist groups repulsed the Chadian military, which had also been constantly disrupted by Tombalbaye's whimsical promotions and demotions. He arrested senior military officers at will and imprisoned them for alleged mutiny.

Meanwhile, FROLINAT's influence had begun to dwindle because of internal conflicts, but the rebels still had a common enemy in Tombalbaye. Provoked by his disrespect, the Chadian Army quickly joined the list of Tombalbaye's enemies.

On April 13th, 1975, Tombalbaye's presidential residence in N'Djamena, the capital of Chad, witnessed a bloody coup. Tombalbaye was shot and killed by men from the aggrieved Chadian Army. Upon hearing the news of his death, the capital erupted in jubilation. The people trooped to the streets to celebrate the death of a tyrant.

The next president of Chad, General Félix Malloum, did not create much change. The rebels, especially the Muslim factions, saw him as being no different from the former president. He resigned in 1979, four years after his appointment, and a transitional government took over for the next three years.

Nonetheless, Chad remained a theater of unending civil unrest between the Northern Muslims and the sub-Saharan Southern Christians. The most recent Chadian Civil War began in 2016, with a coalition rebel group raiding parts of Northern Chad. It is still ongoing as of this writing. Since the 1960s, the bone of contention has not changed; it is unknown if the two sides will ever overcome their deep-rooted ethnic and religious rivalry.

Angola's Civil War

Around the time when Chadian dictator François Tombalbaye was overthrown and killed, massive changes were happening in another coastal area of Central Africa.

In 1975, Angola, one of the first countries in Africa to be colonized by the Portuguese settlers, was reeling under the dictatorship of Marcelo Caetano, the prime minister of Portugal. Noting the trend of independence struggles sweeping through Africa at the time, it was only inevitable that some Angolans would begin to agitate for independence.

Three liberation groups led the independence struggle in Angola: the People's Movement for the Liberation of Angola (MPLA), the National Front for the Liberation of Angola (FNLA), and the National Union for the Total Independence of Angola (UNITA). These groups sprang up in different parts of the country, but they had a common goal—well, that is, until Angola gained independence from Portugal on November 11th, 1975.

The handover was abrupt, caused by a bloodless coup in Portugal that removed the prime minister from power and caused the colonial government to be momentarily distracted. But as long as they had fought to be free from Portugal's control, it appeared as though Angola had no real idea of how to move forward as a united front.

Angola quickly slipped into a bout of civil war, with the three main liberation groups becoming belligerents in a power tussle. The roots of this war were ethnic and ideological clashes between groups forced to live as one during colonial rule.

For instance, the MPLA was based in the urban areas of Angola, and its members had a more nationalist agenda for Angola. The FNLA, on the other hand, did not care for a united Angola. The members of the FNLA were natives of the ancient Kingdom of Kongo in northern Angola, which had been forcefully integrated into the Angolan colony during the partition of Africa. During and after the struggle for independence, the rural-based FNLA members were clear in their demands to have the old kingdom back the way it was, which means they could not accept MPLA's unification agenda. The third group, UNITA, consisted mostly of the rural Ovimbundu ethnic group and shared a similar stance with

FNLA. The two militant rural groups could not stand the urban communist MPLA, much less share an independent country with them.

Another unique aspect of the Angolan Civil War was that it had officially begun before Angola achieved independence. According to historical sources, the three liberation groups had temporarily suspended their differences during the fight for independence, but their alliance was not built to last. With the sudden transition of power to an independent Angola, no structures were left in place by the Portuguese, and none of the liberation groups were directly left in charge.

It all went downhill from there.

On the eve of Angola's independence, the MPLA captured Luanda, the capital, and installed its leader, Agostinho Neto, as the first president of Angola. In his first act as president, Neto declared Angola a one-party state, but this only further enraged the FNLA and UNITA.

The warring groups thought it vital to seek foreign aid to fund their wars. Angola suffered an early economic crisis, partly as a result of colonial exploitation and partly because the liberation groups nearly exhausted Angola's oil and diamond reserves to fund their conflict.

Cuba and the Soviet Union allied with the MPLA, while the United States and South Africa supported FNLA and UNITA, respectively. The FNLA lost its footing in the battle, and UNITA became the MPLA's major opposition. In the years leading up to 1980, MPLA enjoyed the recognition of the Organisation of African Unity (OAU), the Soviet Union, and Cuba. UNITA retained the support of South Africa and, after the collapse of the FNLA, the United States.

The role of the United States and the Soviet Union in the Angolan crisis has been described as an extension of their Cold War conflict. The Soviet Union was the leader of the communist bloc whose interests aligned with the MPLA's party values. The United States supported the FNLA and subsequently UNITA against the communists.

President Neto spent the two years of his presidential tenure quelling endless uprisings and coups. Although the MPLA was recognized by the international community as the legitimate Angolan authority, the citizens of Angola were pro-UNITA. This disunity was a devastating propeller, fanning the flames of civil war. After Neto died of pancreatic cancer in 1979, the MPLA quickly installed an interim administration that facilitated the election of José Eduardo dos Santos as the second president of Angola. Dos Santos would remain in power from 1979 until 2017, making him one of the longest-serving presidents in Africa.

A ceasefire negotiation took place between dos Santos of the MPLA and Jonas Savimbi of UNITA in June 1989. However, it broke down after barely two months. The war blazed on until 2002, when Jonas Savimbi was killed by government troops. The Angolan Civil War was a disruptive series of events that led to the displacement of millions of Angolans, the forced conscription of children, child marriage, and massive migrations from targeted rural areas. Landmines and bombs decimated the civilian population in staggering numbers without any reparations or support for the affected families.

The Angolan Civil War represents a dark period. Angola still grapples with the aftermath, and insurgency is far from being a thing of the past.

Ivory Coast's Civil War

Félix Houphouët-Boigny was not your regular dictator. Unlike the typical hatred and disgust that many dictators stir up in the hearts of their subjects, the people of Ivory Coast respected and adored Boigny. Make no mistake, he ran a very tight ship, but he did not overindulge in violence.

As perhaps the only dictator to ever "win over" the opposition with political wit and pragmatism, Boigny was president from the year of Ivory Coast's independence in 1960 until his death in 1993. He was reelected four times, all unopposed, and his people affectionately called him Papa Houphouët.

Boigny's political genius and charisma led Ivory Coast to prosper economically amid the abject poverty that other African countries lived in after their independence. His idea to develop Ivory Coast's agrarian economy drove up the country's revenue through the export of cocoa, coffee, and palm oil. His free-enterprise policies encouraged foreign investors to contribute to the country's wealth, and Ivory Coast quickly rose to prominence as one of the top free-market economies.

Portrait of President Félix Houphouët-Boigny
https://commons.wikimedia.org/wiki/File:F%C3%A9lix_Houphou%C3%ABt-Boigny_1962-07-16.jpg

Another one of Boigny's lauded accomplishments was his ability to manage ethnic tensions within the country. Despite Ivory Coast's existence as one nation, there was a cultural divide between the Muslim North and the Christian South. A third faction of Ivorians was the descendants of immigrants who had trooped into the country in the wake of its economic success. A majority of these immigrants were Muslims from parts of West Africa. Since the Boigny administration was hospitable to them, their numbers increased to almost 30 percent of the country's population.

The natives were increasingly worried that the immigrants were taking over their land, but the stability of the political sphere assuaged their fears. With the death of beloved President Boigny in 1993, Ivory Coast had to choose a different leader for the first time.

Naturally, the tensions between the multiple groups in the North and in parts of the South worsened.

The next president of Ivory Coast was unable to fill President Boigny's shoes and could not maintain order. Five years into his presidency, he was overthrown by a military regime. Rebel groups had sprung up all over the immigrant-held North against the native South. The native Ivorians would not recognize the immigrants as eligible citizens of the country, which means they didn't believe the immigrants could participate in elections.

The Northern Ivorians continually complained about being mistreated by the natives, but nothing changed. In fact, they were even more sidelined by the military government. A constitutional referendum was held in 2000, shortly before the elections. It was a hurried procedure to change the constitution by barring non-native Ivorians from running for election. This change prevented the infamous non-native aspirant named Alassane Ouattara from running, exacerbating the broiling resentment in the Muslim North.

When Laurent Gbagbo, a native Ivorian, emerged as president, coordinated attacks were launched in many parts of the country. In the first outbreak, former military President Robert Guéï and his family were murdered. Even Alassane Ouattara, a non-native, was attacked.

Laurent Gbagbo
https://commons.wikimedia.org/wiki/File:IC_Gbagbo_Motta_eng_195.jpg

Alassane Ouattara.

The group targeted Gbagbo and demanded a more inclusive redefinition of Ivorian citizenship. With the aid of the French, Ivory Coast's former colonizer, the Gbagbo-led government quelled the first wave of rebellion. It ended with a ceasefire in October, one month after the outbreak.

However, there was more to come. Two new rebel movements, the Movement for Justice and Peace (MJP) and the Ivorian Popular Movement of the Great West (MPIGO), launched an all-out civil war in November 2002.

The French continued to support the Gbagbo-led government until November 2004, when an Ivorian aircraft "accidentally" exploded at a French base in Bouake, Ivory Coast. This explosion, which might have been ordered by President Laurent Gbagbo, killed nine French soldiers and one American. Over thirty others were gravely injured.

Mistake or purposeful (it is possible that Gbagbo ordered the attack but did not mean for anyone to be killed), the French did not take kindly to this attack. France instantly turned against Gbagbo and attacked the Ivorian military airbase in Abidjan and

Yamoussoukro, the capital of Ivory Coast. This act enraged a pro-Gbagbo youth movement known as the Young Patriots. The Young Patriots retaliated by raiding the buildings of French expatriates and destroying their possessions.

France counterattacked by sending a contingent of six hundred troops from Gabon and France. The terrified French nationals were evacuated to their home country on military airplanes, and then the French Army gunned down the Young Patriots, killing an unidentified number of Ivorian youths.

The Ivorian Civil War dragged on until the year 2007. In that year, two peace treaties were signed between the government, represented by Gbagbo, and the rebels, represented by Guillaume Soro.

Ivory Coast enjoyed the next four years of relative peace and stability until the Second Ivorian Civil War broke out in 2010. This time, the conflict was between the incumbent President Laurent Gbagbo and his opponent, Alassane Ouattara, who had been previously sidelined in Ivorian politics.

Ouattara won the 2010 presidential election, but Gbagbo would not step down, alleging that the election results were fraudulent. Ignoring the pressure from the international community and peacekeeping missions, Gbagbo clung to his power while his supporters unleashed sporadic violent acts in cities throughout the country.

Peaceful civilian protesters against the Gbagbo government were shot by Ivorian security forces, and Gbagbo expanded his army by recruiting mercenaries from neighboring countries. When all attempts at a peaceful resolution had dried up, Ouattara's forces began to retaliate violently.

Until the arrest of Gbagbo on April 11th, 2011, Ivory Coast was besieged with gunfights, explosions, and airstrikes. The First and Second Ivorian Civil Wars cost the country a great deal of financial, military, and human resources.

Conclusion

Civil wars, which often resulted from ethnic clashes and disharmony due to colonization, went a long way in robbing many African countries of the political and economic stability they aspired to achieve after independence. These wars, as well as horrific genocides, have left a black mark on African history from the mid-1900s until the present day.

In April 1994, Rwanda, a country in the eastern part of Central Africa, exploded in a bloodbath targeted at the Tutsi tribe. In the course of 100 days, over 800,000 Rwandans were brutally murdered by their fellow citizens of the Hutu tribe. Over 300,000 women were violently raped, and children were killed indiscriminately. Similarly, in Darfur, western Sudan, what is known as the first genocide of the 21st century began in 2003. The genocide had its origins in land ownership disputes between the Arab-speaking pastoral nomads and non-Arab-speaking sedentary farmers of Darfur many years earlier. These disputes degenerated into inter-ethnic wars that formed the background of the Sudanese Civil War in the 1950s and 1960s. Political and religious strife were the immediate causes of the Darfur genocide, and the non-Arab-speaking tribes in the region suffered violent deaths, displacement, and the pillaging of their possessions.

As in Rwanda, rape was mechanized against women and girls, and the civilian population suffered much trauma. Despite the peacekeeping efforts of the international community, the Sudanese genocide persists to date.

The continent of Africa has yet to fully recover from the age of wars, strife, and genocides. Belligerents in the affected regions remain accountable for causing untold havoc to their fellow Africans in the pursuit of their own interests. However, history cites a common pattern in the tragic origins of these conflicts. All of these wars and killings were an offshoot of the political and economic disruption of colonial rule.

Chapter 5 – Dictators and Revolutionaries

In the era before many African countries broke free from colonial domination, a few Africans had their names etched in the histories of revolution. These men and women, typically belonging to the formally or militarily educated African elite, raised the loudest voices against the oppression of European colonizing powers. They founded liberation groups and anti-colonial movements and participated in revolts seeking to end the repression they had known for their entire lives. While names have disappeared in the long, frail pages of history, others remain a common memory across the continent of Africa today.

Similarly, an unforgettable crop of Africans emerged in the post-independence era. A few of them had been revolutionaries during the colonial regimes of their respective countries, forming a part of the first African governments after the Europeans left. In time, however, these Africans proved to be autocratic, brutal, and ruthless in the leadership of their own people.

Would history be kind to these dictators?

Idi Amin of Uganda

On January 25th, 1971, the people of Uganda were thrilled to learn that their president, Milton Obote, had been overthrown in a military coup. Obote was away in Singapore for the first-ever meeting of the Commonwealth Heads of Government Meeting when his estranged ally, Idi Amin, led a coup to oust him from Uganda's seat of power.

As the people rejoiced at Obote's misfortune, they were completely oblivious that their new leader was no better. As a matter of fact, they were in for what was likely the worst eight years of their lives.

The Beginning

After his parents' separation during his childhood, Idi Amin was raised by his mother, Aisha, who belonged to the Lugbara tribe, a central Sudanic ethnic group in parts of Uganda and the Democratic Republic of the Congo. Much of Idi Amin's childhood as the son of a native diviner is shrouded in mystery; he would not even give up the real date that he was born, but historical sources estimate he was born sometime in the 1920s.

His formal education was brief, but this did not hinder his promising military future. As a young man in his twenties, Idi Amin had every desirable physical feature of a soldier. He was recruited to the King's African Rifles in 1946, a regiment of Africans who fought for the British army. A few sources state that he began his military career in the kitchen, where he made meals for soldiers.

In time, Idi Amin's six-foot-four-inch build and natural skills in athletics could not be wasted in the kitchen or running errands in military camps. He was enlisted as a soldier and became popular among his colleagues and superiors for his impressive abilities in rugby and combatant and water sports. Three years after he was recruited, he rose from a base private to a corporal.

The 1950s provided another opportunity for Idi Ami to prove his resourcefulness to the British, which he did to a cruel fault. As part of the detachment sent to curtail the Mau Mau uprising against the British government in Kenya, Idi Amin was notorious for his brutal interrogation methods and extrajudicial killings of his fellow Africans. This was occasionally a source of great concern to the

British government, and there was some debate as to the ripple effects of his lawlessness. Ultimately, the British authorities decided that Idi Amin was a dangerous weapon best kept close. His erratic cruelty aside, he was a talented soldier and had a proven track record of service to the British government.

So, rather than punish Idi Amin, the British government promoted him. By the end of the 1950s, he had risen to the highest attainable African rank in the colonial military: afande class two (warrant officer).

Power for Grabs

Idi Amin must have befriended Milton Obote around the time the latter led the independence struggle in the early 1960s. As a soldier who had actively participated in suppressing anti-colonial struggles in other regions on behalf of the British, it was ironic that Idi Amin would switch sides. It is ironic but not entirely illogical.

For what it was worth, Idi Amin had attained the highest rank an African was allowed in the British military, so no feat could get him any higher. Idi Amin also seemed to have a good knowledge of the times. By 1960, Africa was quickly slipping out of colonialism's grip. It was a timely decision to align with the anti-colonial movement and not get crushed under the crumbling colonial system.

Before Uganda gained independence on October 9th, 1962, the British government commissioned Idi Amin and his men to investigate Turkana cattle thieves from Kenya. Similar to his time in the Mau Mau uprising, Idi Amin and his men did the opposite of investigating. Instead, they captured suspects and tortured them to death or buried them alive. The British government had had enough of Idi Amin's insubordination. After all, Ugandan independence was around the corner, and they'd have no more use for him then.

British government officials ordered the would-be prime minister of Uganda, Milton Obote, to prosecute Idi Amin. However, Obote had other plans for his friend.

Idi Amin was promoted to captain in the independent Uganda Army. He rose to major in 1963, and his partnership with Obote became stronger, thanks to their common military expansionist interests and lucrative smuggling business. The next year, Obote made Idi Amin commander of the Uganda Army. Together, they smuggled ivory, coffee, and gold from the Republic of Congo into Uganda and enriched themselves thoroughly, raising the suspicions of the ceremonial head of Uganda, King Mutebi Mutesa II of Buganda.

Modeled after its colonizer Britain, newly independent Uganda was initially run by a head of government (the prime minister of Uganda). A year later, King Mutesa II was elected president. These two leaders shared political power, but the prime minister was more directly in charge of running state affairs. King Mutesa II of Buganda was Prime Minister Milton Obote's constitutional equal.

One day, in 1965, King Mutesa II called on Parliament to investigate allegations of smuggling against Obote and Idi Amin, his righthand man. In short order, Prime Minister Obote defied Parliament, suspended the constitution, and empowered Idi Amin with the title of commander-in-chief of Uganda's armed forces. With this, Idi Amin's men seized the five members of Parliament who had initiated the investigation and then led a charge to King Mutesa's palace. The king of Buganda fled for his life and remained in exile for the remainder of his days.

With the king of Buganda gone and a new constitution imposed, Obote founded a new political order and made himself the president of Uganda on April 15th, 1966. At the time, Obote had no idea that the man he had set over the most powerful arm of his administration would become his arch-nemesis.

As the highest-ranking officer in the Ugandan Armed Forces, Idi Amin had a wealth of military resources at his disposal. Just like the British during independence, Obote soon outlived his importance to Idi Amin.

The commander started courting his old friends, the British, as well as some Israeli groups, for international support. He also envisioned a private army and began recruiting men from the Kakwa and Lugbara tribes, the native tribes of his parents, to join the Ugandan military.

The news reached Obote that his friend was making shady moves. Obote also discovered that an overwhelming majority of the Uganda Army was loyal to Idi Amin. The last straw was an assassination attempt on President Obote by suspected Idi Amin loyalists. Obote quickly redefined his friendship with Idi Amin and demoted him to commander of only the Uganda Army instead of the combined armed forces.

Animosity brewed rapidly between the two former friends.

Just before President Obote set out on his trip to Singapore in January 1971, he ordered Idi Amin's arrest for the appropriation of army funds. However, the latter had prepared a countermeasure in advance. While Obote was away from Uganda, Idi Amin staged a military coup and captured Kampala, the capital city of Uganda. In a national radio broadcast, Idi Amin declared himself the new president of Uganda, touting himself as a better replacement for the corrupt and ethnic bigot Obote.

Idi Amin gave the people the idea he was in charge of a transient government and promised to step down after the next election. The people accepted the new regime and were further convinced of Idi Amin's intentions when he held a befitting state burial for the exiled king of Buganda and released political prisoners as promised.

Unfortunately for many Ugandan people, that was the last they'd see of Idi Amin's goodwill.

The Despot

It was barely a year after Idi Amin's "caretaker regime" took the seat of power of Uganda. The new head of state had embarked on a radical restructuring of Uganda's politics. He had abandoned the constitution, made himself the chairman of the country's Defense Council, and elevated military officers above civilians in key government positions. He also initiated a violent purge of the Uganda Army, exterminating all of Obote's supporters. Thousands of pro-Obote soldiers fled Uganda when the witch hunt began in 1972, and they rallied around the exiled ex-President Obote to stage a comeback.

Their attempt was a monumental failure, but Idi Amin would not let them go scot-free. His response was a string of violent genocidal actions, targeting the pro-Obote Lango and Acholi ethnic groups. An estimated six thousand soldiers were killed in skirmishes throughout the country.

President Idi Amin.

Gradually, the lines were blurred between the targeted groups and innocent civilians. This was only the beginning, as seven more years of turmoil awaited the Ugandan people. Religious leaders, politicians, key executives of the civil service, students, and academics were murdered indiscriminately, their bodies dumped into the Nile to be devoured by crocodiles.

While the people struggled to adjust to the shocking reality of their despotic leader, the economy of Uganda was crumbling. Idi Amin enjoyed a thoroughly luxurious lifestyle at the country's expense. He resided in a lavishly furnished mansion. And in addition to his six wives, he had over thirty concubines. His men partook in the largesse, with occasional gifts of liquor, cars, promotions, and other incentives to fuel their murderous expeditions on his behalf.

Another blow to the Ugandan economy was Idi Amin's erratic expulsion of the fifty thousand Asian and five hundred Israeli business owners and workers who lived in the country. He accused some of the Asians of being disloyal to Uganda. He believed they had refused to integrate into Ugandan society and risked upsetting the balance of an ethnic Ugandan state.

You probably wonder when and why Idi Amin's relationship with Israel went sour. Remember when Obote and his supporters attempted to overthrow Idi Amin's government? Tanzania was their ally in the fight against Idi Amin. So, when the coup failed, Idi Amin had a score to settle with Tanzania. He launched a series of invasions and requested Israel to supply arms for his retaliation.

Israel refused, and a vindictive man like Idi Amin never forgot. After Israel declined to supply arms, Libya stepped in to grant Idi Amin's request. This was the start of a promising friendship with the Libyan leader, Muammar Gaddafi.

To repay Israel for turning a blind eye in his time of need, the Israeli working-class population in Uganda was given an ultimatum to vacate the country. One of Idi Amin's ministers stated that the reason given for this sudden expulsion was that Idi Amin had a dream about the Israelis posing a threat to Uganda and that he had been directed by God to remove them.

Many of these foreigners owned successful businesses that contributed immensely to Uganda's economy. After forcing them to leave the country, Idi Amin portioned their businesses among his supporters, but their incompetence caused terrible inflation.

Idi Amin was also a famous ritualist who openly bragged about his cannibalism. His image in the international community was of a despicable, murderous bigot; he was worse than the man he had overthrown. Nonetheless, Idi Amin was set in his ways. Like Israel, Britain cut off all ties with Uganda during the peak of Amin's regime, which led him to add the title "Conqueror of the British Empire" to his self-acclaim.

A very distinct aspect of Idi Amin's existence was his double personality. Despite his violently oppressive actions that were telling of his narcissism and delusions of grandeur, he postured excellently as a good leader. He had successfully convinced the entire country of his commitment to better governance. National archives have pictures of him shaking hands courteously with nationals and foreign guests. He was also famous for always smiling and dancing with ordinary citizens. These gestures preserved a positive image of Idi Amin in the minds of certain Ugandans, and not even his most violent crimes against humanity could change that. He could simply do no wrong in their eyes, and their justification for his actions was that he was a strong, decisive leader.

The year 1979 was the last year of Idi Amin's presidency. Tanzania responded to Idi Amin's umpteenth attack on one of its provinces. The Ugandan rebel forces collaborated with Tanzania in this historic counter-offensive. Kampala was heavily occupied.

Idi Amin with King Khalid of Saudi Arabia.
CC0, via Wikimedia Commons;
https://commons.wikimedia.org/wiki/File:Idi_Amin_with_king_khalid.jpg

Idi Amin fled from the capital and sought refuge with his friend, Gaddafi, in Libya. For the next ten years, he remained in hiding, unremorseful for his multiple hate crimes and murders. In 1989, following a futile comeback attempt, he relocated to Saudi Arabia and stayed there until he died of kidney failure.

Between 80,000 and 500,000 people were killed by the Idi Amin regime; he was never prosecuted for his crimes.

The Revolutionary: Nelson Mandela

The Name That Stuck

His name was Rolihlahla, but between the Europeans' inability (or unwillingness) to pronounce the name and the customs at the Methodist School he attended when he was seven, he was given the name Nelson. It stuck.

Nelson Rolihlahla Mandela was the son of a Thembu tribal chief from the Xhosa-speaking Madiba clan. He was born on July 18th, 1918, and grew up in his hometown, Mvezo, located somewhere along the Eastern Cape of South Africa. As royalty during the British colonial rule, Mandela was afforded a better education than the average native.

After his father died, twelve-year-old Mandela came under the guardianship of the next Thembu king, Jongintaba Dalindyebo. He would not see his mother, Noqaphi Nosekeni, for many years, but Nelson was treated kindly by his new guardian and his wife. At the time, Nelson was too young to understand the scope of colonialism, so he had a simple opinion of the Europeans in his country. They were people of goodwill who had brought education and the Gospel to Africa, and their presence had significantly improved the people's lives. Having been baptized at the age of nine, Nelson was raised in a family of Methodist Christians.

Three years after he was adopted by the new Thembu royal family, Nelson moved to the Clarkebury Methodist High School for his secondary education. He dreamed of becoming a privy councilor for the Thembu royal house he had grown up in, but that changed within the next six years. He advanced to the University of Fort Hare in 1939, where he studied English, politics, and anthropology.

Nineteen-year-old Mandela.
https://commons.wikimedia.org/wiki/File:Young_Mandela.jpg

Mandela enjoyed a wide range of physical activities in his youth. He excelled in long-distance running and boxing, and as a college undergraduate, he indulged in ballroom dancing. However, Mandela would not become renowned as a sportsman or dancer. After joining the Students Representative Council (SRC) at the University of Fort Hare in 1940, Mandela was, for the first time, part of what his name would be acclaimed for: the fight for change.

A Monster Named Apartheid

Mandela's name was not the only name that would resound throughout South Africa. Eight years after Mandela was suspended for joining a protest against the low-quality food served to students at Fort Hare, another name would emerge: apartheid.

Back in 1940, after Mandela and his fellow student protesters were punished with suspension for protests organized by the SRC, Mandela returned home to the Mqhekezweni Palace. Upon his arrival, he heard terrifying news of his adoptive father's plans to marry him and Justice, his stepbrother, off.

Marriage was the last thing on Mandela's and Justice's minds, but there was no talking their father out of it. So, they ran away to Johannesburg, the bustling capital of South Africa. It was the first place that Mandela would experience a horror worse than an arranged marriage: blatant racism.

The descendants of the European colonizers in South Africa were in the minority, yet they treated black South Africans with unbridled contempt. In 1943, Mandela enrolled at the University of Witwatersrand for a degree in law. As the only black South African in his class, Mandela was frequently discriminated against. Like other blacks, Mandela was repulsed by the treatment of people based on the color of their skin. Agitations against this racism were the foundations of nationalist movements like the African National Congress (ANC), which became a social democratic party.

The next general election in South Africa was held on May 26th, 1948. However, the black South Africans, who constituted a majority in the country, were excluded from voting. Results were declared based on half of the total white and Asian South African minority vote—barely a fragment of the country's total population.

The conservative National Party came into power with Daniël François Malan as the new prime minister of South Africa. His six-and-a-half-year tenure saw racial discrimination become encoded in the South African constitution. Apartheid emerged, and the non-white people of South Africa would have to wrestle with legalized racism for the next quarter of a century.

Racial segregation was the aim of apartheid, but its reality had more adverse effects. A new social structure was designed, and at the apex were white South Africans, followed by the Indians and the Asians. The Africans were at the bottom of the social chain, despite being the largest population in the country.

The first tenet of apartheid was a ban on mixed-race marriages. Legislation was signed to this effect on July 8th, 1949, prohibiting marriages between whites and non-whites. A year later, the

Immorality Amendment Act was also signed, preventing sexual relations between whites and non-whites. The apartheid government further enforced the segregation of races in housing. Millions of Africans were forced to leave their homes in urban areas for assigned neighborhoods, and the blacks got the worst locations with infertile lands prone to industrial pollution. The Reservation of Separate Amenities Act of 1953 designated the best spots in public parks, buses, hospitals, beaches, and educational institutions to whites only.

Common signposts during the apartheid era
https://commons.wikimedia.org/wiki/File:ApartheidSignEnglishAfrikaans.jpg

Common signposts during the apartheid era
https://commons.wikimedia.org/wiki/File:Apartheid-signs-trainstation.jpg

Colored people could only access certain parts of the country with government-issued IDs, which included details of their names and races. Colored people could not vote or be voted for by the mid-1960s, and the restrictions mounted year after year. The oppressed black South Africans would not just sit and take it.

The Long Walk to Freedom

Nelson Mandela was thirty years old when the apartheid system was made law, and as an active member of the ANC, he joined other activists in demonstrations against apartheid. Strike actions and peaceful protests were initially used to call attention to the systemic cruelty of the white minority population.

However, the response to this was savage crackdowns and police brutality. About eight thousand protesters and black non-protesters were arrested and incarcerated for their "crimes" of defiance against the apartheid government. Mandela became increasingly involved in politics and activism, which cost him three failed final year exams at the University of Witwatersrand and a law degree certificate.

Rather than pro-black Africanist activism, Mandela embraced multi-racial equality and the belief that South Africa could be home to multiple races that could coexist in harmony and mutual respect. His ideals clashed with radical, pro-black activists, but apartheid was their common enemy.

When the apartheid government launched its anti-communist act that was designed to further quell the opposition, Mandela joined Hyman Meir Basner's law firm in Johannesburg. The firm was run by a staunch communist. Mandela began to realize that they had been too pragmatic with an evil government and led other young colored activists to launch a new campaign on June 26th, 1952. It was tagged the Defiance Campaign, and it stood against the repressive laws of the apartheid regime. The execution-style of the Defiance Campaign was civil disobedience, and it was more of an organized series of demonstrations against apartheid. It also included acts of defiance like "trespassing" into white-only areas and showing no remorse when they were arrested and charged.

In the same year, Mandela and an associate activist, Oliver Tambo, founded the first black-owned law firm in the country. They represented the interests of colored people who had been oppressed by apartheid.

All peaceful attempts at getting the apartheid government's attention through the Defiance Campaign were futile. Rather than be overwhelmed by the protesters, the government ordered arrests, imprisonments, and killings. Mandela and his people were branded as insurrectionists, but their Defiance Campaign caught the world's eye, bringing attention to the apartheid regime.

On the Sunday morning of June 26th, 1955, thousands of people assembled in Kliptown, Soweto, for a meeting. There, they listened to the Freedom Charter statement, which declared that all people were equal before the law and deserved equal rights. The congress was dissolved abruptly when the police came, and Mandela and other activists were arrested and arraigned for treason. The trial ebbed on for four and a half years with no tangible progress, and in 1961, Mandela and his associates were found not guilty. In retrospect, the 1956 Treason Trial is regarded as the apartheid government's strategy to keep the opposition distracted from politics.

Meanwhile, another event set off more aggressive anti-apartheid agitations in South Africa: the Sharpeville protest of 1960. Sixty-nine protesters were murdered by the apartheid police, and thousands were detained. Martial law was declared, and the African National Congress and the Pan African Congress were banned. It was a deliberate tactic to seal off the black opposition parties and secure the apartheid regime for the coming elections. The white minorities wanted to stay in power.

After Mandela was released, his law firm was closed, and his associate, Tambo, fled from the country to escape the apartheid regime's shakedown. Now sure that peaceful protests would be ineffective against the government, Mandela resolved to make his advocacy more militant. He went underground, rallying military support from anti-apartheid and pro-communist nations, including the People's Republic of China. He slipped from country to country, skillfully evading the authorities, earning him the alias "Black Pimpernel." He was a master of disguise; for his safety, he had to take on multiple identities to get past immigration authorities.

In 1961, Mandela and two others founded the uMkhonto we Sizwe (Spear of the Nation) as the paramilitary arm of the African National Congress with the mission to end apartheid. A few members of this group were white communists, and they would hide Mandela in their homes. The ideals of the new group were formulated, and Mandela led the armed struggle.

Three years later, Mandela was captured and charged with four counts of sabotage and conspiracy against the government. During his defense, Mandela made an epic statement:

"During my lifetime I have dedicated myself to this struggle of the African people. I have fought against white domination, and I have fought against black domination. I have cherished the ideal of a democratic and free society in which all persons live together in harmony and with equal opportunities. It is an ideal which I hope to live for and to achieve. But if needs be, it is an ideal for which I am prepared to die."

This statement came from the famous "I Am Prepared to Die" speech, and the black people of South Africa would never forget it. Mandela had been famous for his public speaking, rallying, and multiple arrests, but that speech was the ignition for unrelenting advocacy against apartheid. The prosecution requested for Mandela and his associates to be sentenced to death, but the court pronounced life imprisonment instead.

Mandela was sent off to Robben Island, a remote prison mostly for political prisoners, located west of the mainland. The living conditions in Robben Island were tougher for black prisoners. They had fewer food rations than those of other races, and they wore shorts instead of trousers, despite being made to sleep on straw mats in dingy cells. Mandela and the other activists were targeted by the prison wardens for physical and verbal abuse, and his eyesight deteriorated as a result of unprotected exposure to limestone during hard labor.

A replica of Mandela's cell on Robben Island.

The anti-apartheid movement blazed on while Mandela was in prison, with black activists like Steven Biko at the front lines of the resistance in the early 1970s. Unlike Mandela, Biko and other young black anti-apartheid activists cared little for inclusive activism. They believed that colored people, especially the blacks, had borne the brunt of the apartheid and thus, should be the center of the anti-apartheid struggle. Their ideas were manifested in pro-black Africanist campaigns, riots, and protests. Still, the apartheid government pushed back against the opposition. Steven Biko was brutally killed by the police.

Mandela's wife, Winnie Madikizela-Mandela, was another powerful voice against apartheid during her husband's imprisonment. As a member of the African National Congress, she was one of the first people to be detained under the apartheid government's Terrorism Act in the 1960s. She was frequently forced under house arrest, banned from traveling, and arrested and tortured by the police. She actively participated in the Soweto Uprising of 1976, which stood against the imposition of the white South African dialect, Afrikaans, as the official medium of instruction in black schools.

Winnie Mandela

Steven Biko

An estimated twenty thousand black students from various high schools in South Africa joined the march against the repressive law. During the riots, the apartheid government deployed 1,500 armed policemen to attack the unarmed students. The apartheid police killed between two hundred and seven hundred young adults and injured over one thousand. Among the people arrested and imprisoned in connection to the Soweto Uprising was Winnie Mandela. She was banished from her home in Soweto to Brandfort, where she was held in solitude under strict surveillance and under terrible conditions. Despite the ugly scandals that Winnie would later answer to, her influence as a militant anti-apartheid activist in the 1960s and 1970s was astronomical.

Meanwhile, visits to Nelson Mandela in the prison on Robben Island were limited to one person for thirty minutes per year. He could send and receive only two heavily censored letters a year. Still, Mandela did his best to keep up with the outside world by collecting newspaper clippings. After long days at the lime quarry, he'd work on his law degree from the University of Oxford at night. Mandela rejected at least two releases, as their conditions included him giving up his militant advocacy. These rejections made him even more famous while in prison. His fame within the walls of Robben Island increasingly worried the apartheid authorities. So, to prevent him from "influencing" the other prisoners, Mandela was moved to Pollsmoor Prison in the eighteenth year of his imprisonment, where he spent another five years.

In total, Nelson Mandela was in prison for nearly thirty years, but his anti-apartheid advocacy never waned. He corresponded with the African National Congress and other anti-apartheid groups, which began to loudly rally for Mandela's release in the 1980s. The Free Mandela movement attracted thousands of South Africans and international support groups.

The apartheid government began to disintegrate, beginning with a few concessions made in favor of the colored populace by Prime Minister F. K Willem de Klerk's administration. For the first time in over two decades, the African National Congress was unbanned and recognized as a political party. Seventy-one-year-old Mandela, who had completed his law degree, was released unconditionally in February 1990.

The Victory

Celebrations erupted in Cape Town, with thousands taking to the streets to welcome him. He gave a speech at the First National Bank Stadium in Johannesburg to over 100,000 people. There, he called for peace and reconciliation between all races, as well as the end of the apartheid government.

Mandela quickly took to traveling the world to seek international support from countries in Africa, Europe, and the Americas. After a series of intense negotiations with the South African government, the apartheid system was nullified on April 27th, 1994, the same year that the next general election in South Africa was held. For the first time in almost fifty years, colored South Africans exercised their right to vote, and Nelson Rolihlahla Mandela became the first president of South Africa.

President Nelson Mandela.
© *copyright John Mathew Smith, 2001, CC BY-SA 2.0;*
https://commons.wikimedia.org/wiki/File:Nelson_Mandela_1994.jpg

Mandela's administration was committed to undoing the racially discriminatory policies of the apartheid government. Activist prisoners were granted pardons, and economic reforms were passed to fix the racial disparity caused by decades of apartheid. The Mandela government also drafted and institutionalized a new constitution for the Republic of South Africa. The new constitution included the recognition of all races as equal and new political structures for a presidential system of government since South Africa would no longer be led by prime ministers.

Until his death in December 2013, Mandela gave his life to fight for racial equality and human rights. He is often seen as the messiah of South Africa and a father of the nation. He was decorated and given over two hundred awards in his lifetime, including the Nobel Peace Prize, the Presidential Medal of Freedom from the United States, and the Soviet Union's Lenin Peace Prize. His birthday was declared Nelson Mandela International Day by the United Nations in 2009 to commemorate his advocacy.

Nelson Mandela remains in the hearts of many today as a hero of uncommon dimensions.

Conclusion

Notable people have come and gone in African history, and many were either dictators or revolutionaries. Robert Mugabe of Zimbabwe, Muammar al-Gaddafi of Libya, and Samora Machel are other well-known African leaders.

Whether these leaders were on the right or wrong side of history, they were bold—or perhaps audacious—enough to exert radical principles regardless of the cost.

Chapter 6 – African Relations with the US

Interactions between the United States and Africa date back to the 17th century when America was still a colony of Britain. The Native Americans who had previously owned land in most parts of North America had been pushed back by the increasing population of new European settlers. As you know, these settlers were involved in the slave trade. An estimated 10 percent of the slaves stolen from Africa ended up in what would become the United States of America. Many were also shipped to South America and the Caribbean.

In the early 19th century, a controversial statement by President Thomas Jefferson called for the enactment of the Act to Prohibit the Importation of Slaves. This Act "prohibited the transportation and importation of slaves into any place within the United States." In Jefferson's opinion, the act would hasten the termination of the slave trade in America. Jefferson was also famous for his "all men are born equal" slogan amid criticisms against his ownership of slaves.

The slave trade brought hundreds of thousands of Africans to colonial America, and their descendants became the African Americans of the independent United States. Shortly after millions of slaves were freed, some black Americans believed that the United States could never truly be home for them. There was simply no separating the trauma of their former lives and those of their ancestors. Their motivations were a fine blend with those white people who empathized with them and white segregationists who wanted blacks out of their land.

By 1816, a new colony was readied for the freed slaves to start new lives. Not all of the freed blacks subscribed to this; there was no going back to Africa after so many years of displacement. America was the only home they knew, and they were prepared to stay and fight to be recognized as equal citizens. The two opposing sides could not seem to find a place of agreement, but it didn't stop the hopefuls from looking to their new home, Liberia.

The United States and Liberia

When the United States government reportedly approved 100,000 dollars for the establishment of Liberia in 1819, its motives were questioned. Was it a genuine repatriation gesture to the freed slaves, or was it a prelude for subsequent interventions of the United States in Liberia's affairs? Only time would tell.

The freed slaves that went to Liberia (subsequently known as Americo-Liberians) did not meet empty lands or uninhabited spaces. The Kissi and Gola indigenous tribes, who had migrated from north-central Africa in the 12th century, occupied the land. With them were people of the Kru, Mande, Bassa, Kpelle, Mano, and other tribes who lived on the land before the freed slaves.

After the mass migration of freed slaves from America to these regions, the natives were gradually stripped of their land. Liberia was established and sponsored by the United States government, and Liberia quelled the native resistance. This would not be the last of America's involvement in Liberia's internal affairs, though. The capital of Liberia was named Monrovia after US President James Monroe, who brought the Liberian project to reality during his leadership of the US government.

Between 1821 and 1915, the United States sent naval vessels and military aid to the ruling Americo-Liberian minority in their quest to suppress insurrections by indigenous tribes. Liberia's dependency on the United States continued until the late 20th century.

After the First World War, Liberia suffered an economic meltdown, which was worsened by the expulsion of German businesses from the country when the war was declared. The

Germans had been major investors and important trade partners in Liberia. A history of friendly relations with Germany and the United States, who were enemies in the First World War, put Liberia in a dilemma. The best stance to remain in the good books of both Germany and the United States was neutrality, but pressure from the Allied forces, mainly the United States, forced Liberia to pick a side. Liberia chose to side with the United States.

Germany responded to this by attacking Monrovia, and Liberia declared war on Germany in 1918. The United States rewarded Liberia with funds for the war, known as liberty loans. In the aftermath of the war, America commissioned a rubber company, Firestone, to establish a rubber plantation in Liberia in the late 1920s. This plantation would serve as a stream of national revenue in Liberia's time of economic hardship.

The bonds of friendship between the United States and Liberia waxed rather cold during the Second World War but picked up again during the Cold War.

Another notable dimension of the relationship between the United States and Liberia was long-term protection. While the rest of Africa was partitioned in the late 19th century, Liberia remained under the protection of the United States and was thus untouched by European imperialists. This is why Liberia is often erroneously listed as one of the countries in Africa that were never colonized.

Liberia was colonized but not by a European country and not for very long. As of 1847, Liberia was an independent state, but before then, Liberia would rely on the United States for military protection from native uprisings, loans and grants for economic development, and other forms of aid. Bilateral relations continue between the two countries to date.

The United States and Egypt

As it was a colony of the Ottoman Empire from 1517 to 1867 (with a brief period of French rule tucked in there), Egypt seemed to be off-limits to the United States. The Turks controlled every aspect of Egypt's affairs, including foreign relations and the military. In 1882, the British occupied most parts of Egypt. It seems as if the United States was being pushed away from having solid relations with Egypt.

This would continue until the emergence of the Gamal Abdel Nasser administration in independent Egypt in 1954. It's quite obvious why the United States of America, like other emerging world powers in the 1900s, was so interested in Egypt. Historically, Egypt was a strategically important area in North Africa, acting as the gateway to the oil-rich Middle East and the home of the Suez Canal, one of the most important trade routes in the world.

Britain had enjoyed a good number of years as the controller of the Suez Canal; in fact, the "protection" of the canal was the pretext for the British military presence in Egypt. After Britain and France carved out colonies in Egypt in the early 1900s, it took the military intervention of the United States to rid both Egypt and President Abdel Nasser of their presence. Egypt's political victory against the coalition of Israel, Britain, and France was the start of more bilateral relations with the US.

Some perceive the United States' pursuit of bilateral relations with Egypt as a means to subtly control the region. A man like President Abdel Nasser had pro-Soviet communist leanings, which was a sharp contrast to the pro-capitalist ideology in the US. The United States detected this early on, and after Nasser came into power, the United States made a "keep your enemies closer" move by funding aid for Egypt's anti-colonial efforts. Eventually, Nasser's outlook shifted from pro-communism to neutrality. Nonetheless, the United States invested over a billion dollars in military and economic aid to keep Nasser in power.

Nasser and US President Dwight D. Eisenhower.

Egypt's long, bitter history with Israel was another source of concern that drove the United States' interest in Egyptian affairs. Israel was an ally of the United States, and the US was all for peace between the two countries. The stability between the two countries would keep foreign intervention, especially by the communist bloc, at bay. The relationship between the United States and Egypt was often strained by Egypt's communist leanings, which were manifested in its relations with the Soviet Union and China.

Today, the US and Egypt have a partnership. Both want to see peace in the Middle East. Due to Egypt's proximity to the Middle East, it is seen as a desirable ally for national security reasons. However, the overthrow of Egypt's president in 2013 has soured the relationship, with the US cutting military aid, although it still funds money for counterterrorism operations in Egypt.

The United States and Ethiopia

Two days after Christmas in 1903, the United States of America and Ethiopia, represented by US diplomat Robert P. Skinner and Emperor Menelik II of Ethiopia, forged a historic alliance. As one of the United States' oldest friends on the African continent, Ethiopia had its fair share of fallouts, but an overall cordial relationship endured.

Six years after the United States and Ethiopia began their bilateral relations, the American Legation and a US Consulate in Ethiopia's capital were established. As one of the few African countries that were never colonized, Ethiopia constantly had to defend its territorial integrity.

When Italy occupied parts of Ethiopia in the 1930s with a motive to colonize the country, the sitting emperor of Ethiopia, Halie Selassie, was forced into exile. The United States stayed close and did not recognize the Italian occupation of Ethiopia as legitimate. With Emperor Selassie's restoration to the throne of Ethiopia after the Italian occupation was rebuffed, the ties between the United States and Ethiopia strengthened over the next three decades.

When Mengistu Haile Mariam became the head of state in Ethiopia, relations with the United States took a downturn. Unlike his predecessors, Mengistu openly courted communist countries, even though he knew that the United States was stiffly anti-communist. He was also notorious for the Red Terror, a genocide in 1977 that caused thousands of deaths (possibly hundreds of thousands). In response, the United States withdrew the economic aid benefits it had extended to Ethiopia in the past and refused to render military assistance to the Mengistu regime to quell the civil wars in the country.

After Mengistu's removal in 1991, there were significant improvements to Ethiopia's strained relations with the United States. The Peace Corps, an initiative of the United States to support the growth of developing countries around the world, enlisted Ethiopia as one of its most ardent participants. Ethiopia benefits from US Peace Corps actions, and Ethiopia has its own Peace Corps that supports other countries. In the 21st century,

Ethiopia allied with the United States as part of the global war on terror, which was launched after the 9/11 attacks.

The United States continues to invest in education, poverty alleviation, and economic and military development in Ethiopia and other African countries. The United States is the largest humanitarian donor to Ethiopia.

Generally, the post-colonial period marked the beginning of bilateral relations between the United States and many countries in Africa. Before this time, Africa was heavily occupied by European powers, so it was difficult for the United States to step in. As a matter of fact, the United States was a major influencer in the anti-colonial struggle that engulfed Africa in the 1950s.

United States Administration and Africa

While the nature of the United States' relations with Africa has been fairly consistent over the years, the extent has always varied; it really depends on the US president. Despite the existence of a constitution and models of governance, personal dispositions and the circumstances of the times make every administration unique.

The Peace Corps, which represents one of the highlights of America's foreign policies, was brought into existence by President John F. Kennedy, popularly called JFK. The program enlists and disperses thousands of volunteers across professional fields from America to other countries, especially the remote areas of developing countries. It was founded to improve economies and the quality of living for people in developing areas. It was also designed to project a positive image of America to the international community.

Noble as it was, the Peace Corps, which had been in the drafts long before JFK's presidency, had a number of high-profile critics. One of them was President Dwight D. Eisenhower, JFK's predecessor. Eisenhower and others dismissed the Peace Corps as a "juvenile experiment." His viewpoint on a movement that sought to improve relations with other continents, especially Africa, is possibly the reason the notion that Eisenhower "neglected" Africa exists. In reality, President Eisenhower was involved with events in and near Africa, especially the Middle East.

His administration was instrumental in quelling the Suez Canal Crisis of 1956 by defending Egypt against military occupation by the combined forces of Britain, Israel, and France. Subsequently, he also put forward the Eisenhower Doctrine, which encouraged Middle Eastern countries to approach the United States for economic and military aid in the event of an attack from foreign countries, especially the communists. This was in line with the foreign relations policies of the United States, which acted against anti-colonialism and anti-communism efforts, although the doctrine was rather militant in nature. Considering Eisenhower's background in the military, it seems somewhat natural that he did not care for the structure of the Peace Corps.

His successor, John F. Kennedy, was very different.

With the presidential election barely a month away, Senator John F. Kennedy arrived at Ann Arbor, home of the University of Michigan, in the wee hours of October 14th, 1960. It had been a long day, and he had just flown from New York after an intense debate with his opponent from the Republican Party, Vice President Richard Nixon. He was to spend the night in the Union building for a few hours before continuing his campaign in Michigan the next day.

In a historic twist, Senator Kennedy's campaign received word that some ten thousand students from the University of Michigan had been eagerly waiting to meet him. No speeches had been prepared for this, but Senator Kennedy knew just what to talk about.

For many years, conversations about sending young Americans to needy countries for professional, economic, and military reinforcement had been ongoing. That morning, Kennedy used his platform at the University of Michigan to declare his support of an agency dedicated to that. The speech lasted for barely five minutes, but the Peace Corps movement had been born.

Upon Kennedy's inauguration as the thirty-fifth president of the United States, the Peace Corps became one of the highlights of America's foreign policy. The establishment of the Peace Corps on March 1st, 1961, coincided with the period when many African countries had gained independence from colonial rule. It was also an era when the movements for gender and racial equality in the

United States heightened. So, it was only natural that the Peace Corps was fondly welcomed as part of the flourishing American idealism of the 1960s. The Peace Corps received a wealth of support from the American populace, and thousands volunteered to assist developing countries.

By 1966, the Peace Corps had over fifteen thousand active volunteers in fifty-two countries, most of which were in Africa. President Kennedy's agenda had put America in a different light to the world, countering its earlier imperialist reputation. Volunteers were trained before deployment to be better suited to their destinations, and by the 2000s, over 40 percent of the volunteers were dispatched to sub-Saharan Africa. Apart from JFK's idealistic outlook, the Peace Corps was continually criticized for its fatal flaws, notably the ill-treatment of volunteers in their places of deployment. Female volunteers, who were typically in their twenties, reported cases of rape and sexual assault, most of which the Peace Corps poorly handled. Long after the assassination of its patron, President Kennedy, the failures of the Peace Corps are criticized as overshadowing its success in foreign relations.

Ronald Reagan's constructive engagement was another vital definer of the United States' relations with Africa. During his second term as president, South Africa was reeling under apartheid rule. Black South Africans were violently discriminated against while the minority government legalized boundless constitutional rights to the whites.

By the 1980s, the South African apartheid became a world-known phenomenon, and agitations increasingly rose up against it. The United States was one of the most powerful countries in the world and wielded considerable influence, but apparently not enough to impose an end to apartheid on the South African government, at least in Reagan's opinion.

Jimmy Carter, who had been president before Reagan, had taken a distinctive pro-human rights stance against apartheid, which affected the relations between his country and South Africa. After the Soweto Uprising of 1976 ended in the deaths of innocent civilian protesters at the behest of the apartheid government, Carter promulgated a trade embargo on weapons and other materials that could be used to repress the South African protesters. Under

Carter, the United States employed various strategies to rally international pressure on the South African government to end apartheid. As noble as his efforts were, no real progress was made by the end of Carter's one-term tenure.

When Reagan took office, his strategy was nothing like Carter's. Reagan was convinced that sanctions and aggression were no way to break apartheid. Instead, the nature of the United States' relations with South Africa would have a new face: diplomacy. To achieve this, the Reagan administration would use one of the oldest tricks in the book. It was known as constructive engagement: a non-violent, open-dialogue approach that aimed to influence the South African government to eventually discard apartheid. Reagan's administration loosened the sanctions imposed by the previous Carter administration and reached out to the apartheid government for a new relationship. Trade would be the rallying point of this relationship, and gradually, the United States would "woo" the apartheid government into equally recognizing the rights of all South Africans.

Reagan's strategy of constructive engagement boomeranged when the apartheid situation only went from bad to worse. The South African government colloquially "took the carrot" that the Reagan administration gave them and "made a carrot stew with it." Reagan's leniency was taken as protection from international sanctions, and the South African government fully exploited it. Reagan came under fire at home and in the international community for overindulging a racist, violent government.

Ultimately, the United States would resume a stricter position against the apartheid system until it collapsed in 1994.

Conclusion

There has always been some question as to the real motivations for the United States' consistent participation in African affairs. Nonetheless, judging by the United States' advocacies, from its historic abolitionism to anti-colonialism to anti-communism, the United States has been a force for good in its relations with Africa.

Conversely, considering the United States' occasional withdrawals of economic, financial, and military support from any African country that drifted toward communism, even at the expense of innocent citizens, skepticism remains.

In the end, it is correct that, like any other country, the United States conducts foreign relations that are beneficial to its national interests, which puts it beyond the confines of good or bad.

Chapter 7 – Religion in Africa

Africa is a melting pot of many extremely diverse religions, which have affected the course of history and people's lives. Long before the waves of Christianity and Islam spread through the continent, the indigenous religions of Africans had unique features. Do not be mistaken; none of these religions were the same across multiple regions. However, African traditional religions had a common nature.

First was the belief that every natural element had life. The rivers, plants, animals, mountains, rocks, and even the weather all had a spirit and life. This belief made certain tribes in Africa worship whatever element they found to be most primal to their existence. They would pass down these beliefs to their children through oral traditions. They would have rituals, rites, and festivals to celebrate life in these elements and appease the elements to make their lives better.

This belief was named animism by British anthropologist Edward Burnett Tylor in his 1871 book titled *Primitive Culture*. While the concept of animism in this book is referred to as a framework of African traditional religions, some experts interpret it to be a religion itself.

Another common aspect of native African religions was ancestor worship. This was closely related to the idea of animism, only this time, the deceased were worshiped. The people believed that their ancestors assumed a continued supernatural existence after death and would pray to them for favors, blessings, and protection. Outside religious inclinations, veneration of ancestors was important in African clans and families as a means of preserving family values. In parts of West Africa, the people would fondly call themselves by the names of their ancestors in long family pedigrees. Gravesites were common places of ancestral worship, and if you ever went to ancient Egypt, some tombs were as extravagant as palaces.

For many centuries, Africa was home to thousands of ethnic tribes that practiced their indigenous religions without interference or the desire to spread their beliefs. What changed? When? And how? You're about to find out.

Christianity in Africa

A fascinating fact about the spread of Christianity in Africa is that it began in what is now a mostly Islamic region: North Africa.

Around 43 CE, a Christian Evangelist named Mark arrived in Alexandria, Egypt, with what he called the Great Commission. The Great Commission was a charge that had been given by Jesus Christ to his followers to spread the Gospel of his death and resurrection. It was also the basis for a new religion called Christianity.

Mark became the first bishop of the church in Alexandria. Christianity spread slowly in Egypt for the next three centuries and eventually spread outside its borders to places like Carthage and Tunisia. Centuries after, doctrinal differences arose within the church in Alexandria. This stemmed from different interpretations of the nature of Christ and resulted in the division of the Alexandrian church into two factions: the Coptic Orthodox Church and the Greek Orthodox Church.

At the time, Egypt was under the control of the Romans, and some of the emperors before the mid-3rd century had been tolerant or favorably disposed to Christianity.

Things took a new turn when Roman Emperor Gaius Decius ascended to the throne. As a staunch Roman polytheist, Decius was unwilling to continue the legacy of his predecessors. He issued a decree for every person in his empire to make sacrifices to deities on his behalf, knowing full well that it was against Christian beliefs. The Christians refused Decius's decree and were executed for defiance. One of the first martyrs in Decius's persecution was the pope of Rome, Fabian (Fabianus).

Many Christians fled Egypt to escape the purge, and they sought refuge in the deserts to live and pray. Some would return to what was left of their homes after the purge, but others embraced a new life as hermits.

Decius was a nightmare in the Christian world in the 3rd century, but he was no match for Emperor Diocletian (or Diocles) of the early 4th century. Diocletian was also a Roman polytheist, and his persecution of Christians was far more violent. He razed churches and ordered mutilations and brutal executions of Christians throughout his empire.

Emperor Constantine I of Rome would undo the legacy of Diocletian and encourage the freedom of religion in his empire. Similarly, King Ezana of Aksum, an ancient kingdom in northern Ethiopia, made a historic statement by declaring Christianity as the official religion in his kingdom.

The growth of Christianity in North Africa found a formidable obstacle in the emergence of Islam in the 7th century. Only Ethiopia and a few parts of the region kept to Christianity as Islam spread. Other parts of Africa practiced their traditional religion until commercial sailors from Portugal brought Christianity to the shores of sub-Saharan Africa in the 15th century.

You may have heard of Henry the Navigator. He was a famous Portuguese royal who sponsored and embarked on explorations of a world outside of Europe. He happened upon the coasts of West Africa in the 15th century, and trade relations were established. Thenceforth, the Crown of Portugal funded Catholic missions to West Africa. Christian priests would accompany the sailors to West Africa, and in time, a church opened in Elmina, which was located on the Gold Coast (now called Ghana).

Meanwhile, Jesuit missionaries, another Christian group, arrived in Sierra Leone from Denmark. Italy and Spain had missionaries in the Warri and Benin parts of Nigeria by the late 1500s.

However, the Portuguese Christian missions and those of the Dutch from the 15th to the 16th century achieved little success for a variety of reasons. First, they were limited to the coastal areas of West Africa. The natives there were friendlier because of preexisting years of trade, but the inlanders were different. Language and communication barriers aside, the inland natives were firmly committed to their beliefs and violently resisted change. Second, the interior of Africa was almost impenetrable. The weather there was different, and unlike the natives, the Europeans were not compatible with the harsh tropical weather. Tropical diseases were a deathly risk awaiting anyone who ventured past the coast, and the limited number of missionaries did not help matters. Finally, interest clashes and rivalry among the European countries who wanted parts of Africa for themselves proved to be a major obstacle.

It would take the deliberate, coordinated venture into the interior of Africa by a horde of Christian missionaries from multiple European countries in the 19th century to change the status quo. The Christian missionaries of this era participated in the abolition movement against the slave trade. By then, European ties with Africa had become almost inextricable. Christians from Europe and America poured into Africa, dedicated to the conversion of souls and the expansion of the church. This 18th- to 19th-century movement was led by the Protestant Anglican and Methodist Churches and later the Roman Catholic Church.

For the most part, the slave trade was abolished in the early 1800s, and freed slaves who settled in Liberia and Sierra Leone served as reinforcements to the missionary endeavor. West Africa proved the most fertile ground for the growth of Christianity. In East and Central Africa, the Church Missionary Society (CMS) was introduced in 1844 and extended to Uganda and Tanganyika by 1878. The wider Christianity spread, the more denominations flocked to Africa.

Post-colonial Africa launched the final phase of immortalizing Christianity by "Africanizing" it. In this era, African Christians began to break away from the European-model churches to establish a new order of indigenous Christian churches. The origin of this movement was perhaps the African vision to be free from European influence, which was in alignment with the spirit of the independence era.

The native African churches that sprang up fused non-contradictory elements of the indigenous African culture/religion with Christianity to make a distinctive order. Apart from seemingly defiant motivations, these native churches were made to appeal to the rural populations in African countries. From Christian sermons delivered in native languages to divine healing crusades that simulated the elaborate traditional healing rituals in many African cultures, these native churches were very effective in evangelism. Some of the earliest churches were the United Native African Church founded in 1891, the United African Methodist Church in 1816, the National Baptist Church in Ghana in 1925, the Nigritian Fellowship in 1907, and the Zion Church in South Africa in 1915.

In the years to come, African Pentecostal churches would join the scene and make up the largest Christian community in the world.

Islam in Africa

Sometime in the 7th century, a group of foreigners arrived at the Kingdom of Aksum in modern-day Ethiopia. They were tired yet somewhat relieved that they had fled from the persecution in Mecca to save their lives.

They were the first followers of Prophet Muhammad to perform the Hijrah (Hegira or "flight"). They were received by King Najashi, ruler of Aksum, and allowed to practice their religion under his protection. This migration would give rise to the growth and spread of Islam throughout the African continent.

After the death of Prophet Muhammad in 632, Islam became a powerful movement in Mecca itself. Although the earliest Muslims had faced ridicule and violence in the Arabian Peninsula, Islam became one of the region's biggest exports after the leading clan of Mecca converted to Islam.

The conquest of Egypt by Arab General Amr ibn al-As was another milestone in the spread of Islam. Alexandria was captured in the name of Islam, and the religion spread toward Libya and Tunisia, pushing back the wave of Christianity that had earlier been established.

North Africa was more receptive to Islam than Christianity, even though the latter had come earlier. As Muslims spread across what would become known as the Maghreb, it reached Morocco, Mauritania, and Algeria. The natives who lived in these regions before the advent of Islam were called the Berbers. The Berbers initially resisted the infiltration of an Arabic religion into their lands, but they soon converted.

Before the Arabs took over North Africa from the native Berbers, much of the region was controlled by the Byzantine Empire. Islam clashed against the Byzantine Empire's Christianity. Many kings in North Africa converted to Islam, as did their kingdoms. Islam spread even wider during the Muslims' successive conquests. Apart from warfare, Islam was more attractive to the people living in the Maghreb because of its agreeable doctrines. Polygamy, the use of protective amulets, and other practices were already a part of North African culture, so the religion was quite adaptable.

The next and perhaps most significant phase in the spread of Islam was trade. In the 8th century, the converted North Africans set out into the interior of the continent for trade relations with communities in the east and west. The empires of Ghana, Mali, Kanem, Songhai, and Fulani near the Sahara were the next to accept Islam. The wealthy traders from the north made Muslims their contacts, and a demographic of native Muslim clerics advanced inward with the new religion. The 14th century saw the near-complete circle of Islamization in many parts of the eastern and western coastal areas, as well as the desert trade areas.

Historians opine that the spread of Islam was a way of aligning with the trends of commerce. Also, the religion encoded a set of ethical values for commercial networking, all of which unified believers across trade areas. Where Islam was not completely accepted, it would be tolerated for the advantage of trade.

By the dawn of the 15th century, Islam had become much more than a language of trade. It became a unifier of empires and peoples because it entwined with the cultural lives of believers. Despite the relative steadiness that Islam's growth enjoyed, it was not accepted everywhere. Christianity and other native traditions posed a great obstacle for Islam in East Africa and many parts of West Africa. It took the imposition of the Mamluks of Egypt for Islam to be accepted in the regions of what used to be Aksum and Nubia.

Despite the pressure, the Kingdom of Abyssinia in modern-day Ethiopia remained unshaken in the Christian faith. Colonial rule by Christian imperialists also hampered the spread of Islam in sub-Saharan West Africa, save for a few communities.

The influence of Islam in African history is represented in clothing, architecture, literacy, education, and much more.

Other Religions in Africa

Indeed, Christianity and Islam were unopposed in the extent of their influence on the history of Africa, but other religions had a formidable impact. For a continent with thousands of ethnic tribes, religious diversity was a crux of ancient Africa's existence.

In the late 19th century, the British Empire spread rapidly through the continent, imposing colonial authority over the natives in sub-Saharan Africa and some parts of North Africa, but the Europeans were not the only foreign settlers in the land. There was an influx of Indians who worked for the Europeans as indentured laborers and were barely treated any better than the African natives. The Indians populated eastern and southern Africa more than West Africa, and they brought Hinduism with them.

Unlike Christianity or Islam, Hinduism did not seek to convert other people unless they willingly decided to embrace it. This might have accounted for why the religion did not spread or compete against Christianity and Islam, despite its similarities to many African traditional religions. Another important factor was the resistance of African Christians and Muslims against the few attempts to spread Hinduism in post-colonial Africa.

Despite being the third-largest religion in the world, Hinduism in Africa has remained a small flame. Half of Mauritius's population, a country in East Africa, is made up of Hindus. More recently, there has been a small movement for Hinduism in Ghana.

Like Hinduism, Buddhism and Zoroastrianism adherents are mostly of Asian descent, with very few African converts. Most of these converts live in parts of Uganda, Zambia, Lesotho, Kenya, Zanzibar, and Ghana.

When talking about religion in Africa, an interesting observation stands out.

Until the advent of Islam and Christianity, the continent of Africa was hardly embroiled in religious clashes. There would be inter-ethnic wars and political rivalry, but religion was not a point of conflict. Many African traditional religions were non-proselytizing, meaning they did not seek to convert non-adherents. Traditional religion and culture were inseparable in ancient African communities, so a typical African traditional religion could not fit into cultures outside those of its adherents. The greatest empires in ancient Africa could annex smaller kingdoms politically and transform the political structures of their tributary kingdoms all they wanted, but religion was often never interfered with.

Christianity and Islam, foreign exports, would change that, and it would begin centuries of an endless divide between the two major religious groups. This divide would breed intolerance and fan the flames of rivalry, with one group desperate to dominate the other. This would be the pretext for many civil wars and ethnic clashes in many parts of post-colonial Africa.

Chapter 8 – Modern-day Africa: The Reality

The "Third World" is a blanket term used to refer to developing countries of the world—or, in reality, "under-developed" countries. As home to 33.3 percent of the poorest people in the world, Africa has been the poster continent for the "Third World" for as long as we can remember.

The continent has also suffered, from slavery to colonial rule, to a barrage of civil wars. Through it all, the reality of Africa as we know it has overarching themes of hope and hopelessness in unequal proportions.

Which one is more prominent?

The Challenges

Despite the growth of Africa's economy over the past generations, the disparity between the poor and the rich is a wide chasm. When the 21st century began, African countries like Angola, Nigeria, Ethiopia, Equatorial Guinea, Rwanda, and Mozambique were appraised as budding economies; however, most of them have been knocked off the trail of steady economic development. Nigeria was declared the poverty capital of the world in 2018, with nearly ninety million people living in extreme poverty. Half of Guinea and Mozambique's population live below the poverty line, while Rwanda has yet to recover from the 1994 genocide and the civil wars that followed.

Economic inequality is what happens when a country's wealth is not evenly distributed to all its citizens. The wealth of Africa has never been in question; Europeans exploited Africa's resources for hundreds of years during colonial rule and could not exhaust them. The challenge lies in what should be accessible to all. The exclusivity of wealth in Africa has pushed millions down the poverty line, and the conditions have worsened in recent years.

In an assessment of the Southern African Customs Union reported by the World Bank in March 2022, it was revealed that South Africa is the most unequal country in the world. This is a direct legacy of the tortuous apartheid regime that plagued South Africa for forty-six years. Central Africa comes a close second, followed by West Africa. The concentration of wealth in the hands of the minority has come with high rates of economic inequality, posing a challenge to the distribution of wealth. For instance, 0.0001 percent of the minority in South Africa own at least 70 percent of the nation's wealth.

These discrepancies go as far back in African history as the 1950s and 1960s. The first post-colonial African elites envisioned taking over from the Europeans to exploit their fellow citizens. It became rampant among politicians and public servants, including those who had been nationalists, to misappropriate funds and amass wealth with public resources.

This weaves into another unfortunate trend in modern Africa— the continued desecration of fundamental human rights.

In history, Africans greatly suffered, with their rights being trampled on by foreigners who partitioned and took over their land. Subsequently, it became a reason for nationalists and pan-African freedom fighters to band together to demand independence.

Ironically, the events that followed after independence were intra-African bloody struggles for the recognition of rights. From Nigeria to Rwanda, South Africa, and even the Middle East, successive civil wars played out involving the horrific, blatant trampling of Africans' rights. These stemmed from the idea that a certain demographic, whether religious or ethnic, was superior to others. Africa is still grappling with such crises, and economic resources drained by these skirmishes are yet to be replenished in many nations.

The Rwandan Genocide: A Case Study

On April 6th, 1994, President Juvénal Habyarimana of Rwanda and visiting President Cyprien Ntaryamira of Burundi were killed in a plane crash in Kigali, the capital of Rwanda. The plane had been shot down, which meant that it was calculated murder.

A few hours after the deaths of everyone aboard the plane, the streets of Rwanda turned red with the blood of hundreds of thousands more people, people who were murdered with impunity. It was the beginning of the one-hundred-day Rwanda genocide, from which the country has yet to recover.

Historically, Rwanda was home to three major tribes: the Hutu, the Tutsi, and the Twa (who first occupied the region that became Rwanda). The Hutu were the largest in number, yet their Tutsi counterparts were favored during colonial rule. The Tutsi were allowed better job opportunities and were generally treated better by the Belgians than any other tribe because the Tutsi had lighter skin and similar physical attributes to the white Europeans. Fearing that the colonizers would transfer the leadership of independent Rwanda to the minority Tutsis, the Hutus declared war in 1959, three years before Rwanda would gain independence from Belgium.

Over 300,000 Tutsis fled for their lives during the Hutu revolution, and the Hutus installed one of their one, General Habyarimana, as the leader of independent Rwanda. The Tutsi refugees sought asylum in Uganda, a neighboring country, where they lived for many decades. Their descendants formed a political movement called the Rwandan Patriotic Force (RPF) and invaded Rwanda in the 1990s. Hutu President Habyarimana retaliated against the Tutsis who lived in Rwanda by ordering their deaths for being accomplices of the RPF.

Three years after, the killings and arrests stopped, and President Habyarimana announced that the next government of Rwanda would include the Tutsis' RPF. Unfortunately, he did not live to actualize it. He was murdered, and no culprits were caught or tried. Some people named Hutu culprits who hated seeing the Tutsis come to power as the murderers, while others thought it was the RPF.

On the same day the Rwandan president was killed, the Hutu organized into militia groups and took to the streets, mounting roadblocks and killing Tutsis on sight. Government officials were not spared from the massacre. The prime minister of Rwanda, a moderate Hutu woman named Agathe Uwilingiyimana, was killed, along with other moderate Hutu cabinet members who might hamper the genocide.

Belgian peacekeepers were dispatched to Rwanda, but many were killed. In response, the Belgian government removed its troops, leaving the helpless Tutsis to their fate. Murders engulfed the country. The vacuum in leadership was occupied by Hutu extremists who used the media to propagate their anti-Tutsi agenda. Ordinary Hutu citizens were ordered to slaughter their Tutsi neighbors and rape Tutsi women or be killed instead. Tutsi settlements were raided, and inhabitants, no matter their age or gender, were killed violently. Hutu and Twa moderates who refused to participate in the madness were killed. For three months, the purge continued, and by its end in June 1994, the death toll was at an estimated 800,000. Some believe that over a million people were killed. It remains one of the bloodiest events in African history.

Clothes of the murdered victims in a Catholic church in Nyamata, Rwanda.
Adam Jones from Kelowna, BC, Canada, CC BY 2.0
<https://creativecommons.org/licenses/by/2.0>, via Wikimedia Commons;
https://commons.wikimedia.org/wiki/File:Interior_of_Catholic_Church_Genocide_Memo rial_Site_with_Piled_Clothes_of_Victims_-_Nyamata_-_Rwanda.jpg

The survivors of this genocide would suffer the trauma of watching their fellow civilians being shot or hacked to death. Some of them were forced to take part in inflicting death and suffering on their friends and neighbors. In a 2013 mental health study, survivors showed high tendencies of mental health deterioration and psychotic challenges caused by the genocide and life in refugee camps.

Almost 100,000 confused children were separated from their parents, and families were decimated. According to World Vision, a humanitarian aid organization, "it was clear that children needed more than physical help. Healing work started right in 1994 when children were showing signs of trauma."

There were also environmental consequences of the war. Houses, churches, and public buildings were razed or destroyed, farms were pillaged, and the water systems were polluted. The putrid odor of blood must have lingered in the air for some time, and the next government of Rwanda would allot a chunk of the nation's revenue to rebuilding.

Twenty-eight years after the Rwandan genocide, the country still reels from it. In the early 2000s, the Rwandan government embarked on an industrialization agenda, and President Paul Kagame announced his plans to make Rwanda the "Singapore of Africa." According to metrics, however, the events of 1994 depleted the country's economic and human resources, so efforts geared at reviving Rwanda have not been a complete success. About 39 percent of the Rwandan population lived below the poverty line in 2015.

The Menace of Sweatshops: Another Case Study

Sweatshop. It's in the name.

You can imagine it. Hundreds of workers crammed in a tiny space, leaning over equipment and sweating profusely as they work for hours on end for little pay.

The first sweatshop can be dated back to the 19th century, around the time that the slave trade was abolished in most European countries and colonies. The introduction of machinery enabled many industries to increase their production capacity. One of these industries was textile making.

As thousands trooped to urban areas like London, Paris, and New York in search of ways to make a living, a league of business owners in garment districts developed an exploitative system. Sweatshops spread throughout the urban centers of Europe, recruiting thousands of desperate women and men into the most ruthless variants of cheap labor, perhaps second only to slavery.

A group of women in a sweatshop in New York, 1908.
https://commons.wikimedia.org/wiki/File:Group_of_women_in_sweatshop_of_Mr._Sentr ei,_87_Ridge_Street_04457v.jpg

In English Professor Charles Kingsley's expose on the menace, he tells the stories of workers in sweatshops and the despicable work conditions they endured:

"One sweater I worked with had four children and six men, and they, together with his wife, sister-in-law, and himself, all lived in two rooms, the largest of which was about eight feet by ten. We worked in the smallest room and slept there as well—all six of us. There were two turn-up beds in it, and we slept three in a bed. There was no chimney, and, indeed, no ventilation whatever. I was near losing my life there the foul air of so many people working all day in the place, and sleeping there at night, was quite suffocating. Almost all the men were consumptive, and I myself attended the dispensary for disease of the lungs. The room in which we all slept was not more than six feet square. We were all sick and weak, and loth to work. Each of the six of us paid 2s. 6d [two shillings, 6 pence] a week for our lodging, or 15 shillings altogether."

Needless to say, most of these workers were immigrants and included Africans. The sweaters (employers) would occasionally force women to take birth control medication and undergo pregnancy tests to prevent them from getting pregnant. They also fired women who got pregnant.

Sweatshops became more popular in the late 1800s and extended beyond the garment-making industry. The term "sweatshop" became applicable to any work environment where workers were subjected to harsh neglect and terrible conditions. By the 1910s, several anti-sweatshop unions had sprung up throughout Europe, and criticisms arose against the exploitation of labor. This led many governments in Europe to draft and implement labor regulations.

By the 21st century, the sweatshop system transformed into an ugly extension of neocolonialism and slavery in Third World countries. Popular brands around the world established sweatshops in Africa under the guise of industrialization and the creation of job opportunities.

In March 2022, *TIME* magazine uncovered a sweatshop scandal involving renowned AI intelligence company Sama. In the feature story, the Sama office in Nairobi, Kenya, recruited almost two hundred young Africans as content moderators for Facebook. The shocking reality, however, was that they were clustered up in tiny offices, denied their rights to unionize, and paid a meager $1.50 per hour.

Their job to remove graphic or offensive content from social media platforms was, in the words of a former employee, "a kind of mental torture." Some employees resigned after being diagnosed with anxiety, depression, and post-traumatic stress disorder (PTSD). It was also revealed that Sama gagged worker protests and fired employees who attempted to rally for strike actions. Sama denied these allegations, but legal actions are still in order against the corporation for breaking labor laws.

This is just one of the many instances of the sweatshop menace in Africa. It is certainly a cause for concern.

Child labor, one of the worst offshoots of the sweatshop system, is prevalent in Africa. It all began with the enslavement of children in Africa, Europe, and the Americas. The slave trade did not spare children from hard labor on plantations, mines, domestic households, and construction sites. Even today, the use of underage children for domestic labor, mostly unpaid, persists.

Children born into poverty are at a higher risk of being given away, sold, or trafficked into child labor. According to the metrics of the past decade, an estimated 72.1 million African children are victims of child labor. The numbers keep shooting up in sub-Saharan Africa, where millions of children are drop-outs or uneducated. In parts of Nigeria, Rwanda, Morocco, Kenya, Madagascar, Ghana, and other African countries, child laborers become victims of sexual harassment and rape.

Exploitative labor is the bane of Africa's existence because of the rate of abject poverty in the continent. For people who are doomed to starve if they don't work to make a living, being victims of harsh, dehumanizing work conditions for a trifling amount is better than nothing.

Humanitarian Aid in Africa

Humanitarian aid in Africa was inevitable. The continent had seen the inflow of many foreigners from as early as the 7th century, and relations wove into trade and colonialism, which characterize Africa's history with foreign powers.

It has been argued that Africa is entitled to all the aid it can get from the international community, especially from countries that "ruined" the economies of African countries and disrupted the political structures of ancient Africa. Humanitarian efforts in many parts of Africa have been consistent since their inception. The first humanitarians in African history would be the missionaries, who brought not only the Gospel but also education and healthcare.

Post-colonial Africa has hosted many governmental and non-governmental humanitarian organizations. In nearly every story of civil war, genocide, or internal conflict in African history, you will find at least one humanitarian group was present to help alleviate the fallout.

After the Rwandan genocide, organizations, such as the United States Agency for International Development (USAID) and World Vision, sent field teams to provide emergency humanitarian aid. While World Vision focused on rehabilitating the survivors through healing exercises and helping to rebuild displaced families, USAID supported Rwanda's political and economic recovery for the next five years, giving an estimated $61 million in aid.

Organizations like Concern Worldwide, which was established by a small group of humanitarians in 1968, have been of notable assistance to Africa. Concern Worldwide was an initiative by a group of Irish Christians in response to the dire need for aid in Biafra during the Nigerian Civil War. Igbo men, women, and children of Biafra lived in extreme hunger after their access to food was cut off by the Nigerian government. Concern Worldwide reached out to the Biafrans with food supplies and medicine. After that, it offered aid to eastern Pakistan, Haiti, and fifty other countries. An estimated thirty million people have benefited from this organization.

Similarly, Trócaire was established in the 1970s by the Catholic Church in Ireland to combat social and political injustices by raising funds for victims. The organization offered aid to the starving civilians in Ethiopia and Somalia in the 1980s and 1990s when the regions were embroiled in conflict.

Conclusion

You have read about the ugly side of the African continent, but it does not mean Africa's future is bleak.

Africa has undoubtedly been through very harsh times, with each generation struggling to overcome layers of prejudice, racial hatred, and inter-ethnic clashes at home and abroad. The continent went from being the home of homogenous tribal communities that took much pride in their tradition and culture to a breeding ground for ruthless slavers and imperialists who disrupted the existing structures and altered the course of history forever. Throughout it all, the peoples of Africa have survived every bout and risen from the ashes.

As the holder of the world's most abundant natural and mineral resources, the continent of Africa is indispensable to the global economy. As a people with a history of refusing to bow to oppression, the Africans are the epitome of bravery and laudable resilience. More Africans live under democratic systems today than at any other point in history, which has contributed immensely to world peace.

Since the mid-2010s, many countries in Africa have enjoyed political stability, a crucial element of a developing country. The year 2017 was noted as the least violent year in Africa since the post-independent era began in the 1950s. Nations that have been at war since time immemorial are gradually conceding to peace. In East Africa, Eritrea and Ethiopia put to rest their border conflict in 2018 and signed a lasting peace pact. As part of the pact, the two countries agreed to forge intimate cooperation. Ever since, the two countries have strengthened their alliance and better coexisted in peace.

The African Union replaced the Organization of African Unity in 2002 and has since embarked on multiple missions to secure a united Africa. The African Union has been a force for change by mediating conflicts in Somalia, Darfur, Libya, Mauritania, Mali, and many other countries. This union has held its own for the entirety of its existence and has recorded success in many campaigns.

Africa has also shown good promise in its handling of global pandemics, notably Ebola in 2014 and 2015 and the COVID pandemic that began in 2020. In Nigeria, the most populated country in Africa, the Ebola virus was swiftly contained after the government ordered the tracking of all contacts with the index patient. It was a race against time, but with the dedication of fearless medics and the Nigerian citizenry, the virus was contained within two months.

Finally, the long list of Africans who are making strides in the global community as leaders of industries, key executives, and academics cannot be ignored. Following in the footsteps of revolutionaries like Thomas Sankara of Burkina Faso, Patrice Lumumba of Congo, Funmilayo Ransome-Kuti of Nigeria, and Nelson Mandela of South Africa, many Africans have emerged as front liners in world politics, art, and leadership.

It has been a long, rocky road for the continent, but the new generation of Africans who inherited the determination and strength of the ones before them continue bravely onward. From all indications, Africa can and will make a full recovery from history's bruises.

Here's another book by Captivating History that you might like

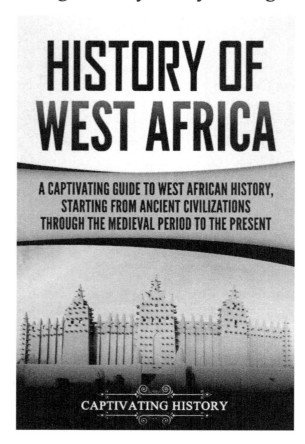

Free Bonus from Captivating History: History Ebook

Hi History Lovers!

My name is Matt Clayton, and I'm the creator of Captivating History. First off, I want to THANK YOU for reading our books in the Captivating History series. As an avid reader of History myself, I aim to produce books that will hold you captive.

Now you have a chance to join our exclusive history list so you can get the ebook below for free as well as discounts and a potential to get more history books for free! Simply click the link below to join.

P.S. If you join now, you will also receive a free Mythology book. Remember that it's 100% free to join the list.

Captivatinghistory.com/ebook

Also, make sure to follow us on Facebook, Twitter and Youtube by searching for Captivating History.

Bibliography

• Smitha, Frank E. "Africa and Empire in the 1880s and '90s." *www.fsmitha.com*. Retrieved 2019-12-19.

• Oliver, R. (ed). *The Cambridge History of Africa, Vol. 3.* Cambridge University Press, 2001.

• Borrero, Mauricio (2009). *Russia: A Reference Guide from the Renaissance to the Present.* Infobase Publishing. pp. 69–70.

• "From Crime to Coercion: Policing Dissent in Abeokuta, Nigeria, 1900–1940." The Journal of Imperial and Commonwealth History. 47 (3): 474–489. doi:10.1080/03086534.2019.1576833. ISSN 0308-6534. S2CID 159124664.

• Brantlinger, Patrick (1985). "Victorians and Africans: The Genealogy of the Myth of the Dark Continent." Critical Inquiry. 12 (1): 166–203. doi:10.1086/448326. JSTOR 1343467. S2CID 161311164.

• Hunt, Lynn. *The Making of the West: Volume C.* Bedford: St. Martin, 2009.

• Hobson, John Atkinson (2011). *Imperialism.* Cambridge: Cambridge University Press. p. 77. ISBN 978-0-511-79207-6. OCLC 889962491.

• Langer, William A. Bureau of International Research of Harvard University and Radcliffe College (1935).

• The Diplomacy of Imperialism, 1890–1902. Vol. 1. New York and London: Alfred A Knopf.

• Arendt, Hannah. *The Origins of Totalitarianism.* Schocken, 2004. ISBN 0805242252

- Hobsbawm, Eric. *The Age of Empire.* NY: Pantheon Books, 1987. ISBN 0394563190

- Darwin, John. "Imperialism and the Victorians: The Dynamics of Territorial Expansion." Hobson, J.A.

- *Imperialism, A Study.* Cosimo Classics, 2005. ISBN 978-1596052505

- Lindqvist, Sven. *Exterminate All the Brutes: A Modern Odyssey into the Heart of Darkness.* NY: New Press, 1996. ISBN 9781565840027

- Pakenham, Thomas. *The Scramble for Africa: White Man's Conquest of the Dark Continent from 1876 to 1912.* (1991).

- Aldrich, Robert. *Greater France: A History of French Overseas Expansion.* (1996).

- A. A. Madiebo. *The Nigerian Revolution and the Biafra War.* (Enugu: Fourth Dimension Publishing Co., 1980).

- Millin, S. Gertrude. *Rhodes.* Chatto & Windus, 1936. ASIN B0026WOV5A

- Pakenham, Thomas. *The Scramble for Africa.* New York: Random House/Abacus, 1991. ISBN 0349104492.

- Petringa, Maria. Brazza. *A Life for Africa.* Bloomington, IN: AuthorHouse, 2006. ISBN 978-1425911980.

- Rodney, Walter. *How Europe Underdeveloped Africa.* African Tree Press, 2014 (original 1972). ISBN 978-1592325948

- Shillington, Kevin. *Encyclopedia of African History.* (New York: Fitzroy Dearborn, 2004)

- Kwarteng, Kwasi (2012). *Ghosts of Empire: Britain's Legacies in the Modern World (1st ed.).* New York: Perseus Books Group. ISBN 978-1-61039-120-7.

- J. O. G. Achuzia. *Requiem Biafra.* (Enugu: Fourth Dimension Publishing Co., 1986)

- "Flora Shaw." The Orlando Project. Cambridge University Press.

- Peach, Lucinda Joy. "Human Rights, Religion, and (Sexual) Slavery." The Annual of the Society of Christian Ethics 20 (2000): 65–87. Print.

- Hrbek, I. (ed). *UNESCO General History of Africa, Vol. III, Abridged Edition.* University of California Press, 1992.

- Vink, Markus. "'The World's Oldest Trade'": Dutch Slavery and Slave Trade in the Indian Ocean in the Seventeenth Century." Journal of World History 14.2 (2003): 131–77. Print.

- Gershowitz, Suzanne (20 March 2007). "The Last King of Scotland, Idi Amin, and the United Nations." Archived from the original on 6 June 2009. Retrieved 8 August 2009.

- Lucas, Scott. W. *Divided We Stand: Britain, the US and the Suez Crisis.* (Hodder and Stoughton, 1991)

- "Garment Industry: Efforts to Address the Prevalence and Conditions of Sweatshops." Government Accountability Office. Archived (PDF) from the original on February 25, 2021.

- Hoda Gamal Abdel Nasser. *Britain and the Egyptian Nationalist Movement 1936-1952.* by (Ithaca Press, 1994)

- Kyle, Keith. *Suez.* (Weidenfeld and Nicholson, 1991)

- Subramanian, Archana (6 August 2015). "Asian expulsion." The Hindu.

- "Idi Amin: A Byword for Brutality." News24. 21 July 2003.

- Turner, Barry. *Suez 1956.* (Hodder and Stoughton, 2006)

- Curtin, P. *African History.* Pearson, 1995.

- Fage, J.D. (ed). *The Cambridge History of Africa, Vol. 2.* Cambridge University Press, 2001.

- Insoll, T. "The Archaeology of Islam in Sub-Saharan Africa." Journal of World Prehistory, Vol. 10, No. 4 (December 1996), pp. 439-504.

- Ward, Kevin, and Brian Stanley, eds. *The Church Mission Society and World Christianity, 1799-1999* (Eerdmans, 2000).

- Ki-Zerbo, J. (ed). *UNESCO General History of Africa, Vol. IV, Abridged Edition.* University of California Press, 1998.

- McEvedy, C. *The Penguin Atlas of African History.* Penguin Books, 1996.

- Department of the Arts of Africa, Oceania, and the Americas. "The Trans-Saharan Gold Trade (7th–14th Century Century)." In Heilbrunn Timeline of Art History.

- Ogot, B.A. (ed). *UNESCO General History of Africa, Vol. V, Abridged Edition.* University of California Press, 1999.

Printed in Great Britain
by Amazon

22587217R00069